Making Friends

A Spanish Memoir

Adam Lowell

Text copyright ©2015 Adam Lowell

Author's Note

All the events described in this little book of reminiscences are as I remember them and all the people in it existed, and mostly still do. Some of their names have been changed out of consideration for their loved ones, past or present, and the names of one or two establishments have also been modified.

Many conversations took place in the Spanish language and in an effort to avoid the usual infelicities of partial translation all speech has been rendered into plain English, except in rare cases where the idiosyncrasy of expression makes reproduction of the original words worthwhile.

1

True knowledge of the bars and pubs in the Infante area of Murcia, c.2000 A.D., cannot begin until one has met Dominic. He was thirty-four then and his incessant energy belied the fact that he'd lost a lung as a result of a car accident. He reminded me of Dean Moriarty in *On the Road* and I told him so, by way of an ice-breaker. He hadn't read it – or much else, I was later to discover – but he asked me to describe him. We were almost alone in the air-conditioned Coyote pub on a hot Sunday afternoon and I told him about the two guys who drove right across America and back just for the hell of it.

His constant nodding suggested that he was interested in the subject, so I told him what I remembered about the content and spirit of the book. He nodded some more and then spoke.

"Have you seen my car?"

"I've only just seen you."

"Come on."

"I haven't paid."

"Never mind." He swung round on his stool. "Juanma," he said to the tall, lean young man behind the bar, "we'll be back."

"No doubt," said Juanma, the owner or the owner's son, depending on who you spoke to, and we were gone.

I followed Dominic along the tree-lined walkway down the middle of Juan Ramón Jiménez Street and marvelled at his sense of purpose on that most aimless afternoon of the week. His hair was short and stylish with just a hint of grey, his face lean and chiselled, and his eyes, I saw when I finally got into stride with him, were brown, slightly bloodshot and somewhat fanatical. He was dressed in a black t-shirt and blue jeans and his body looked powerful, but was nothing compared to the two-lunged version he showed me in a photograph later in the day. We reached his car and he clicked open the doors with a flourish.

"A BMW 525i. I used to have a Renault 5 Turbo that was the talk of Infante in its day," he said, motioning me to enter. "But I'm older now so this is more suitable."

"It's very nice. Where are we going?"

"To the beach."

"Right. Don't we need swimming things?"

"What? No, let's go."

He drove slowly down the avenue and made his way sedately towards the motorway, steering with one hand pressed against the wheel and talking all the while. He turned on the CD player.

"This song is by the Marañones, a group from Murcia, very famous at one time, not just in Murcia."

"It's good," I said, and it wasn't bad.

"A three piece rock group. Pedrín's the drummer. A good friend of mine. Miguel's the singer. He's a good friend of Santiago who used to be in M-Clan."

"I've heard of them. Is Santiago your friend too?"

"A friend of a friend really, but I know where he lives."

"Right."

"Do you want to go there now?"

"No, the beach sounds good."

"I'm Dominic," he said, offering me his hand as he gunned the car along the motorway slip road and straight into the outside lane.

"I'm Adam." I gave his hand the briefest of squeezes and felt my body sink into the upholstery. After such a leisurely exit from the city the speed was a shock but Dominic held the wheel lightly with one hand and produced and lit a cigarette with the other. He offered me the packet of Fortuna.

"No thanks. I don't smoke."

"I shouldn't."

"What do you do?" I asked, immediately realising that it was a very English thing to say.

"My job? I work in the electrical supplies shop at the end of the street we were on. I practically run it. Good place to meet girls."

"An electrical supply shop?"

"Yes. Their dads and husbands send them there. I like women."

"Me too. Have you got a girlfriend?"

"Not right now. There was one, but she caused me to crash the car, so that's over."

It transpired that he had crashed the car we were in, not badly, driving along a country lane alone and drunk one night, lamenting the girl's inconstancy.

"The repair cost a fortune. She was a cokehead too. Never trust a cokehead."

"I won't."

"I used to take it," he said, turning to face me and flaring his ample nostrils, "but I stopped. Too expensive and it made me excitable."

By this time we had passed over the low cordillera that flanks the city and were heading along the flatlands towards the coast. He seemed to have slowed down a little after the curves of the descent and I looked at the speedo. 160 kilometres per hours. That explained why the other cars seemed to be going so slowly. In no time we were off the dual carriageway and driving, slowly again, into the seaside town of Lo Pagán. He pulled up outside a pub very similar to those of the Infante strip that we had left half an hour earlier and we got out. I smelt the sea air but couldn't see it and when the soundproof doors had closed behind us the smell of cigarette smoke predominated.

"A gin and tonic, Paco," Dominic said to the barman over the din of pop music. "What are you having?"

"Just a beer, please."

"It's funny, I only feel like gin and tonic when I'm at the beach. It's good to get out of Murcia sometimes." He lit a cigarette and offered me one.

"I still don't smoke," I said, patting his shoulder. I'm not normally so tactile with people I don't know well, but I thought it might increase his awareness of me. Perhaps it worked.

"What sort of work do you do?" he asked.

"I teach English. Private classes. I sometimes work in a friend's bar too."

"Good morning, Vietnam," he said in English, like in the film. "So you're not from round here?"

"No, I'm English. I've been here, in Murcia, for about two years. I lived in Valencia before that."

At that point people almost always complemented me on my excellent Spanish. Dominic asked me if I knew La Bomba bar. I said I didn't.

"No? It's across from Coyote, in the corner of that little square. It's a rock bar, the best in Murcia. I have many friends there, such as Pedrín, the drummer. I've taken up drumming too. Pedrín is teaching me. We can go to La Bomba later, and perhaps to Pedrín's studio too."

"Studio?"

"Well. More of a rehearsal room, really, in a building with other rehearsal rooms. Pedrín doesn't have to pay for his."

"Oh, because he's so well known?"

"Yes, and because he hasn't got any money."

"Right. Do you want another drink?"

Dominic looked at his half empty glass and swished the ice cubes round. "No, we ought to be getting back." He finished the drink. "Come on."

I finished my beer and followed him out of the heavy doors into the heat and the blinding light. I smelt the sea again. "Are we not going to have a look at the sea now we're here?"

"What? Oh, some other time." He started the car as I was opening my door and in half an hour we were parked on the Infante strip again.

I ought to explain what the Infante strip is. Infante Juan Manuel is the avenue that borders the river across from the city centre and gives its name to the mostly residential zone to the east of the older Barrio del Carmen area. Calle Juan Ramón Jiménez is a wide street that runs roughly south from the avenue and on which several ground floors of the apartment buildings are occupied by mostly windowless and mercifully soundproofed pubs. The Infante strip is my terminology, by the way. It is normally referred to as plain Infante.

Some foreigners who work or study in Murcia visit the Infante strip, normally once, and British people are apt to describe it as a 'townie' area. I had sought sanctuary in the cool, dimly lit Coyote pub that Sunday afternoon in late August in order to get out of my stifling top floor flat in the Barrio del Carmen. A beer an hour was a small price to pay for the relief provided by the barrage of air conditioning units lined up above the entrance and an acquaintance had told me that the music was acceptable.

It was not to the Coyote that Dominic led me when we left the car, however, but into the square opposite where I saw only a few closed shops and several parked cars. In the far corner I discerned the words 'La Bomba' on a small sign above a large metal door. It could have been a fireworks, joke or porn shop, but whatever it was it looked and sounded closed.

"It looks closed," I said as we marched with great urgency towards the door.

"Just wait." He pulled opened the heavy door and waved me into a poorly lit, musty and silent bar. A pale, youngish man with long curly hair and a goatee beard looked up from the foil-wrapped baguette he was eating.

"Qué pasa, picha?" he said to me, which I understood as, 'What's up, dick, or dickhead?' but I was sure he couldn't mean that. "Ah, Dominic, you here already, picha?"

"Is this a bar or what?" Dominic said. "Music, maestro, and drinks for me and my friend!"

"Are you not going to introduce me?" he asked as he screwed up the tinfoil.

"Yes, Troco, this is…"

"Adam," I said quickly, sensing that he had forgotten.

"Adam, yes, this is Troco, owner of the best rock bar in Murcia, when he can be bothered to put music on."

"Picha, I've just arrived." He switched on the music system and put on some Spanish rock music, not too loud. He drank some water and then proceeded to roll a joint with great dexterity.

"Adam is…," Dominic began, but paused until he remembered something about me. "Adam is an English teacher."

"Ah, in one of the language schools?" Troco asked.

"No, I teach private classes. I sometimes work in my friend's bar too."

He lit the joint and smoked appreciatively, keeping most of the emissions on his side of the bar. "Your Spanish is very good, picha. Which bar is that then?"

"It's in the tascas, but it hasn't got a name. It's known as Jed's bar. He's the owner, an American."

"What sort of bar is it?" he asked, his big, brown eyes becoming a little watery.

"Oh, just a bar, you know. He plays good music and it's mainly students and foreigners who go there," I said, which seemed a fair description of the small, nondescript place in the narrow streets to the east of the cathedral, home to many other small bars and pubs.

"Does he play rock music?" Troco asked.

"Mostly."

"You must bring people who like good music here in the evenings, picha. I have concerts most weeks," he said, the effects of the joint not diminishing his business sense.

"We'll go there now," said Dominic, standing up. "And we'll bring some people back," he added, glancing at Troco.

"His wife won't let him open on Sundays," I said.

"But you work there," Dominic said. "Have you got the keys?"

"Yes, but I rest on Sundays too."

"Take it easy, Dominic, and have a drink," said Troco.

Dominic looked around the empty bar and leant his hands on the bar stool in front of him.

"Do you want a gin and tonic?" I asked him.

"What? No, just a beer."

I ordered two beers and was pleased that La Bomba was becoming just as cool as the Coyote. It was almost seven and I'd soon be able to go home and open the windows of my flat. We sat on bar stools and sipped our beer. Dominic lit a cigarette and offered Troco one.

"Not for me. Disgusting habit," he said, before passing under the end of the bar with a dustpan and brush. As he busied himself at the other end of the narrow, tableless room I gathered from Dominic's rapidly tapping foot that he was restless. Unused to his silence I strove for something to say.

"Do you live in the city," was the best I could do.

"Yes, with my mother in San Andrés."

"Do you mind that, living with your mother?"

"My mother is old and needs me. The flat is now mine, though. Let's go back to the Coyote," he said under his breath.

Within a couple of minutes we had finished our beers. I asked Troco, who was still sweeping, how much I owed him and left the coins on the bar.

"I hope to see you again, Adam," he said after propping the brush against the wall and approaching. I held out my hand, but he lifted his and grasped mine at chest height, like all hip people do. "Bring some friends and I'll play some good music. Adiós, picha."

We left the bar and a revitalised Dominic strode briskly towards the Coyote pub.

"Ah, I hate it there when it's so quiet," he said, springing across the first lane of the avenue in a small gap between oncoming traffic.

I didn't catch the rest of the sentence as I had waited for the cars to pass. When we entered the Coyote an REM song was playing loudly and many of the stools around the rectangular central bar were occupied, mostly by young men. We found a space and I noticed that Juanma had been joined by an older, stouter version of himself and a pretty young barmaid.

"Ah, Dominic," said Juanma Jr. "Are you going to pay for this afternoon's drinks?"

I extracted my wallet from my back pocket, but Dominic motioned it away. He tossed a 10,000 Peseta note onto the bar and ordered two more beers. Juanma's handsome, vacuous face registered slight annoyance and he went to fetch the change.

"It's mostly blokes in here," I said.

"Yes, more girls will come in later, but I'm sick of that type of girl." He lit a cigarette.

"What type of girl?"

"Oh, common, uneducated girls who drink and smoke too much. I want to meet some different ones. When does your friend's bar open?"

"Every night of the week except today, but it'll be quiet until Thursday. On Thursdays I help him out."

"Good, on Thursday I will come."

"Yes, do."

"Come and look," he said, and led me over to a photo display on the wall. There were scores of photos, mostly of groups of people in the pub, all posing in attitudes of great gaiety. "There I am, and there, and here. Can you see how strong I was in this one? That was before my accident."

"The one you mentioned before?"

"No, that was nothing. Five years ago, no, six, I crashed my Renault Five Turbo into a wall. No seatbelt. Five fractured ribs and they had to remove one of my lungs."

"It's lucky it wasn't both."

"Yes." He nodded gravely three or four times before slapping his forehead. "Ha, that's your English humour. Very good."

"You still look pretty strong though."

"Yes, but look, look at that photo. I was like a bull," he said, getting quite excited.

"Perhaps you shouldn't smoke."

"I shouldn't smoke, but I do. Ha, I like you, Adam," he said, leading the way back to our bar stools. "Juanma! Two whiskies with cola, please."

"I ought to be getting home," I said, my Sunday habits prevailing over my sense of adventure. It was the first time that I had actually met a habitué of the Infante strip, after all. "But I do fancy a whisky," I added, correcting the faux pas that had made him look momentarily glum.

"I too normally take it easy on Sundays. I have to use this tomorrow." He pointed to his forehead.

"Me too. I have a morning class with a banker. His English is good and he asks difficult questions."

"Yes, I've taken up drumming," he said, tapping the bar rapidly with his fingers and thumbs.

"How's it going?" I asked, not minding that he'd ignored my reference to the banker as I didn't want to talk or think about that fastidious man.

"Very well. Pedrín says I'm making good progress." He twisted his bottle round in his hand. "Pedrín may be in La Bomba by now."

"Right."

"But he may not be."

"No."

"When we finish these we could do one thing."

"What's that?"

"We leave here. You go into La Bomba. If Pedrín is there, you stay. If not, you say you're looking for me and come out again. I'll wait in the square."

"Right, I don't mind doing that, but how will I know if Pedrín is there?"

"You can't miss him."

"Yes, but what does he look like?"

"Long hair, apart from on top where there is very little. A big beard. His two front teeth are missing. Rather pale and not very tall. His eyes are-"

"Right, I think I'll know him." I took a deliberately small sip of my drink and set it back down on the bar. I was in no hurry and very little time had elapsed since we were last in Troco's bar. Dominic finished his drink and stood up. I made the rest of my drink last at least a minute before I got off my stool and followed Dominic out of the door.

When I opened the door to La Bomba, Troco's only customer was a big-boned girl with short hair and thick glasses. I felt foolish asking about Dominic's whereabouts so soon after leaving, but he flashed his fine teeth in a wide smile and moved his head from side to side.

"No, picha, I haven't seen him. Have you lost him already?"

"Yes, I'll see you another day," I said, having decided not to re-enter the place again that evening, come what may.

I found Dominic hiding ineffectually behind a slim tree trunk, smoking.

"No Pedrín?" he asked.

"No."

"Anybody else?"

"Just a big girl with short hair."

"Oh, that will be Chelo," he said with a grimace. "We can try again later."

"No, Dominic, I'm not going back there again tonight." He nodded quickly and made to cross the street. "And I'm not going back into the Coyote now either. How about a bite to eat?"

"Eat? What for?"

"Well, because I'm hungry and we've been drinking quite a bit."

"I can't eat when I'm drinking. It upsets my stomach. Look, let's just have one more drink. I have to go soon."

"Ok. Where?" I asked. Dominic looked wistfully at the door of the Coyote. "How about showing me another of these Infante pubs?"

"They're all awful. I used to frequent them all but they're very vulgar."

"Let's go to the least bad one."

He scratched his nose and tapped his foot. "I'll show you one and we'll have a drink in another."

"Right, lead the way."

We crossed the street and entered a pub two doors down from the Coyote where two doormen were deemed necessary on a Sunday evening. Dominic held open the inner door and ushered me through it. A blast of some kind of techno music hit me as I entered and beheld a central bar like that of the Coyote, but with young people two or three deep around it, all engaging in animated conversation or dancing on the spot. I turned to face Dominic, who was smiling and bopping up and down in a demented fashion.

"Do you like it?" he asked, making robotic movements with his arms.

"No."

"Come on." He spun around on his heels and left. After exchanging a few jocular words with the doormen he led the way along the street. "We'll go to David's pub. It's not too bad."

"Do you think those people in there will be working tomorrow?" I asked, banging my left ear to try to stop the ringing.

"Of course. I used to go there every Sunday."

"They must have bad Mondays."

"Yes, unless they have a little coke or some pills left over to help them through the day."

"Is that what they're on?"

"Yes, and alcohol, of course. This is David's pub."

We had reached the end of that section of the street and entered a pub with windows. The music was low, the upholstery shabby, and the dozen or so customers were seated sedately at the long bar down one side of the room.

"This is more like it," I said. "Do you want another whisky and coke?"

"Ok." After greeting David, a stocky, fit-looking man of thirty, he leant over towards me. "I don't like this pub much," he said.

"Why's that?"

"Drugs and whores."

"Where?"

"Now, I don't know, but dealers come here, and whores too – not to work but to relax," he whispered in my ear.

"Well, why shouldn't the girls have a drink somewhere?" I asked, scanning the bar for possible candidates. I'd never spoken to a prostitute in my life, or if I had I hadn't known it.

"They charge a lot."

"But if they're not working?"

Dominic, elbows on bar, wrung his hands together and began to speak as if to a child. "Yes, well, they're not working, but if a possible customer appears they might go with him."

"So?"

"So, if one is feeling... hot, and one has money in one's pocket, one can be a poor man for the rest of the week."

"Does that happen to you?"

"No, not me." He shook his head vigorously. "No, never, hardly ever. Just twice, in fact, but I don't believe that a man should need to go with a whore."

"A bit of self-restraint then."

"The flesh is weak. Look at that guy down the bar," he said, pointing to a tall, lean, dark-haired man dressed in black who appeared to have arranged some kind of altar in front of him on the bar. His face wore an expression of great concentration as he arranged his possessions around his bottle of beer. I saw a penknife, a wallet, a small metal receptacle, a pipe, several lighters standing upright and a tall glass with a rose in it.

"Do you know him?" I asked.

"No. He goes in the Coyote too. He's crazy," he said, shaking his head sadly.

"Have you ever spoken to him?"

"No, no, he's crazy."

Resisting the impulse to ask him if he thought it might be catching, I instead vaunted my English tolerance for diversity. "He looks harmless enough. If you spoke to him you might find him saner than you think."

Dominic snorted and downed half of his drink. "Crazy."

"He's probably just lonely. Shall we go over?"

"No!" He shuddered theatrically.

"Ok, only joking. I'll speak to him myself some other time."

Dominic finished his drink and looked at his watch. "I'm going to La Bomba now," he said with decision.

"I'm going to head off home and grab something to eat."

"Right," he said, studying the blank wall over the bar.

"I'll see you some other night. On Thursday at Jed's bar if you like."

"Ah yes," he said, suddenly roused. "David! A pen and some paper, please."

"Here you are, sir," David said with a mock subservience that was lost on my new friend.

Dominic tore off a strip of the paper and wrote quickly. "Here is my number… Adam. If you need anything at all, I'm at your service. Now, please draw a little map to indicate where this Jed's bar is, please."

"Do you not know the tascas?" I asked, sure that I would be able to describe the bar's location to a native of the city.

"I go there very seldom. I've been a man of this side of the river, until now."

I drew a makeshift map which he examined.

"I think I know it. If not, I can ask. I'll see you on Thursday at about nine o'clock."

"Ok. Do you not go out any other night?" I asked, being accustomed to having a drink or two after my last class of the evening.

"I never go out during the week. I'll make an exception this Thursday as I think we're going to be great friends."

"I hope so," I said, feeling pleased, in my merry state, to have met someone so different from my friends and acquaintances.

After a traditional low handshake he patted me on the shoulder and shot through the door. While I slowly finished my drink I stole glances at the eccentric man along the bar, but, my Monday morning banker student flashing before my eyes, I decided to save him for another outing. I already had plenty to write in my diary for one day.

2

From Dominic's description I recognised Pedrín immediately when I walked into La Bomba three evenings later. The fact that he was the only customer made introductions seem inevitable, but first I greeted Troco.

"Picha, how's it going?" he responded, offering his hand high across the bar so I'd remember how to grasp it.

"I'm well. Did Dominic come back on Sunday?"

"Yes, two or three times. His music master wasn't here," he said, indicating Pedrín with a nod of the head, "so he couldn't settle."

"Did he drink much more?" I asked, thinking about my own delicate state on Monday morning and my irksome class with the banker.

"Oh, yes. We won't see him again until the weekend. Adam, this is Pedrín, a good friend of mine."

I clasped his raised hand and said hello. He was exactly as Dominic had described him and made no effort to hide his missing teeth when he spoke.

"Pleased to meet you, Adam," he said in a voice more cultivated than his appearance had led me to expect. His beard was dark and thick, but his greying ponytailed hair sparse and his watery blue eyes showed both sensitivity and dissipation. He looked about forty-five, but I had a feeling he was a little younger.

"I believe you are a drummer?"

"I am."

"Picha, Pedrín is one of the best drummers in Spain. When he sits in with the next band who play here you'll see," said Troco.

"I don't know much about music," I said, "but I like it."

Pedrín smiled benignly and took a tiny sip from his almost empty bottle of beer.

"A beer please, Troco. Would you like another, Pedrín?"

"That's very kind of you. Yes, I will."

Troco looked pleased as he uncapped the bottles and set them in front of us. We were silent while Troco rolled a joint, lit it, and walked over to a hatch in the wall that was ajar.

"I believe you're teaching Dominic how to play the drums," I said to Pedrín.

"Yes," he said, nodding solemnly. "We've had a few classes."

"How's he doing?"

"He shows promise, for a man of his age, but his disappearance during the week makes progress slow."

"So he has classes at the weekend?"

"Yes, sometimes two or three, sometimes none."

It would later be revealed to me that Pedrín counted very much on Dominic's 2000 peseta per class payments as they were his only source of income. His band, the Marañones, had not performed for some time and as he hadn't paid much tax over the years he wasn't entitled to any benefits. He lived with his mother in an old flat just over the river.

When Troco had half smoked his joint he leant out of the hatch to view the square before handing it to Pedrín, who smoked appreciatively for a while before offering it to me.

"No thanks, I don't smoke," I said, hoping he realised that I meant marijuana and cannabis, although as I didn't smoke cigarettes either it didn't really matter.

Pedrín didn't mind and smoked the joint right down to the cardboard filter. He sipped his beer and turned to me.

"So, what do you dedicate yourself to, Adam?" he asked.

"I'm an English teacher. Private classes. Not very interesting, really," I said, imagining a younger Pedrín with a thick mane of hair, a full set of teeth, and a crowd of adoring fans stretching back from the stage, rocking to his relentless beat.

"But you make enough to live, don't you?"

"Yes, I do all right, although it's quieter in summer," I said. I didn't say that I made so much money during the year that I could well afford to spend July and half of August in England, tramping the fells and drinking in the local pubs.

Pedrín wasn't forthcoming about his own employment situation, so I didn't ask. It was hard to know what to talk about and Troco wasn't much help. He looked restless, probably due to the dearth of customers.

"How long have you had the bar, Troco?" I asked him.

"Almost two years. It's always quiet in August, but the show must go on," he said, perhaps reading my thoughts. He turned to the music system that had been playing a mixture of Spanish rock songs, a few of which I recognised. He inserted a CD and turned up the volume.

"This is Pedrín's group," he said. "What do you think?"

I listened to the singer's rasping voice, the tasteful but unambitious guitar solos, and especially to the firm beat of the drums. I listened to the song without speaking, waiting for a drum solo.

"Do you not play solos?" I asked Pedrín when the song had ended.

"Not in the studio, sometimes in concert. The drummer's job is to keep the beat."

"Right. Would you like another beer?"

"Yes, but I won't be able to return the favour today."

"That doesn't matter." I ordered two beers and decided to make mine my last. I often struggle with three-way conversations, especially with people I don't know very well, and I don't think either of them really knew what to say to a foreign language teacher. The air conditioning was still whirring away and I wondered how much money Troco would lose that day. At least I'd saved him the cost price of a couple of beers.

The music grew on me though. The songs' lyrics seemed sincere and the guitar, bass and drums meshed well together, but I could see, or rather hear, why they hadn't made it big.

"Do you have any concerts lined up?" I asked Pedrín.

"Not at the moment. Miguel, the singer and guitarist, teams up with Santiago, from another group, to play blues music and they're very busy playing small concerts all over Spain," he said with no trace of resentment in his voice.

"Could you not play with other people too?"

"I could – I do occasionally – but I prefer to wait," he said with a patient smile.

When I'd finished the beer I took my leave, promising to return soon, and strolled past the parked cars to the avenue. I'd only been to La Bomba twice – three times if you count my flying visit – but I already felt disloyal about going into the Coyote pub across the street. I decided to have a quick one anyway.

The Coyote seemed quiet too, but there's a lot of space around that bar and I counted eleven other customers, one of whom was the odd man who had been in David's pub on Sunday night. I seated myself at the far end of the bar, at right angles to him, and ordered a beer from Juanma Jr. who was alone behind the bar.

"Hello," he said with a smile, or maybe a leer, on his face. "Where's your friend today?"

"Dominic? At home, I believe."

"Yes, after Sunday he'll need to rest."

"Yes, I suppose so." I didn't feel like continuing the conversation, so I sipped my beer instead.

"Have you known him long?" he persevered.

"Not long."

"He's a case."

"I don't know him very well."

"On Sunday night he ended up very drunk. A friend had to assist him to his car. He must have had a very bad day on Monday," he said, clearly revelling in the thought of his suffering.

"I guess so," I said. I took my wallet out to pay, having decided that my beer was to be the last of the night. I felt a certain aversion toward that swarthy, thick-lipped man of about my own age – twenty-eight at the time – and decided that an early night was in order.

"No, this one's on me," he said, waving the wallet away and sauntering away to speak to another customer.

Shrewd move, I thought, and turned my attention to the odd man. He had assembled a similar altar to Sunday's in front of him on the bar, with the addition of a pair of sunglasses clipped onto the tall glass containing the rose, and from my position I could observe him undetected. His steady gaze rarely rose from his collection of articles and when he finally ordered another beer he did so by merely lifting his finger when Juanma looked his way. The owner looked at me when he turned away with the empty bottle and raised his eyes. I smiled politely and looked at my watch.

When I ordered my inevitable second beer Juanma asked me if I wanted to hear any particular songs.

"Er, well, you played the Dylan song Hurricane on Sunday. Could you play that?" I said, fortuitously as it turned out.

The odd man's response on hearing the opening bars was to look at me with a broad, lingering smile, before turning once more to his objects. Realising that the acknowledgement was unlikely to be repeated, I picked up my bottle and moved to the stool next to his.

"Hello, how's it going?" I said, reasoning that the two yards between us would mitigate the rebuff that I half expected.

He turned his head slowly. "Hello, friend," he said, with a sleepy smile this time.

His big brown eyes were great pools of something. Disenchantment? Mystery? Madness?

"Do you like Dylan?" I asked.

"Is that who it is? I just like the sound of the violin."

Feeling that small talk would get me nowhere, I risked a more direct approach. "All those things there on the bar, what do they mean?"

"Mean? Well I don't suppose they mean anything much," he said in a deep, pleasant, slightly drawling voice. "They help me to concentrate, I suppose."

"On what?"

"On what? Now that is a difficult question, friend."

He turned back to his things and removed the sunglasses from the glass. He clipped them back on the other way round and contemplated his modification, chin in hand, as if playing chess. Thinking the conversation was over I swivelled slightly towards the bar and picked up my bottle.

"Cigarette?" he said, producing a packet from the top pocket of his black suede jacket.

"No thanks."

"You are not from Murcia," he asserted rather than asked.

"No, I'm English. I've been in Murcia for two years and I was in Valencia for three years before that. I'm Adam."

He offered me his large hand which I just reached from my stool. "Antonio. Pleased to meet you."

I dragged my stool a little closer and sat at forty-five degrees to the bar, facing him.

"Your Spanish is good," he said, having also turned his stool towards me slightly. "What do you do in Murcia?"

"I teach English, like most foreigners, I guess. And you?"

"Unfortunately I am incapable of work at the moment. I receive a small payment because of my condition."

"What's that?" I asked, rather boldly, I thought.

"Well, the doctors cannot quite define it. They thought I might be a manic depressive, but have decided that I'm not that."

"Don't they call that bipolar disorder nowadays?"

"Yes, but whatever they call it, it's not what I have. It's not psychosis either, or schizophrenia. Depression is a factor, they say, but it's more than that. They have simply concluded that my mental health is not good and they give me tablets."

"Antidepressants?"

"Mainly, yes, but I don't always take them."

"Is that wise?"

"I must be master of my own body, Adam. Would you like another beer?"

"I'll get them," I said.

"No." He took out a well-stocked wallet to emphasise the point. "Juanma, two beers, please."

Juanma replaced our empties and I didn't allow him to catch my eye. From his body language I deduced that he found our liaison amusing.

"You seem to be a friendly guy, Antonio," I said. "Don't you think having all those things on the bar will put people off talking to you."

"There is method in my madness," he said, putting on the sunglasses and smiling at me.

"Meaning?"

He took off the sunglasses and put them in his inside pocket. "I don't like people to bother me. I spend many hours sitting in this bar and others, drinking and smoking a little, and I do not want to talk about football or cars or listen to other people's woman troubles. I especially dislike the people who come here and take cocaine. They are insupportable and talk only nonsense."

"Do people do that here?"

"You may be a little naïve, Adam. Why do you think the toilet cistern has a stainless steel cover?"

"I thought it was to stop people breaking it."

"Ostensibly, yes, but its real purpose you can guess."

"Right. I've never taken it. Have you?"

"A few times in the past, but it didn't agree with me. I do like to smoke an occasional joint though." He smiled at the thought. "I find that it calms me considerably."

"Do you ever go to La Bomba?"

His face clouded. "I have been, but will never return." He lit a cigarette and pulled an ashtray up alongside his objects.

"Why's that?"

He took a long pull on his cigarette and exhaled slowly. "When I entered La Bomba there were only two other people in the bar, besides the owner. After ordering a drink I arranged my things as I usually do and asked him for a tall glass for my rose. Then the imbecile said, 'Picha, don't get all your things out on my bar.' I left my beer and left that place immediately. Who the devil calls people 'picha' the first time they meet them, or ever, for that matter?" He put down his cigarette and took a sip of beer.

"I'd never heard the word used like that before," I said.

"Ach, only ignorant people from the villages say it."

"He was all right with me."

"Because you are normal. An advantage of my little eccentricities is that it dissuades stupid people, like Juanma here, from bothering me. A disadvantage of it, in the case of La Bomba, is that I know that he sometimes allows people to smoke joints there. Still, there are plenty of places in the tascas where one can do that." He smiled and slowly finished his cigarette. "All this," he went on, waving his hand over his belongings, "is a filter."

"A filter?"

"Think about it."

I thought about it. "Oh, like a people filter, you mean?"

"Exactly. This way I meet few people, but interesting ones."

"Oh, I'm not that interesting," I said, with sincere modesty, because I don't consider having gained a mediocre Spanish and French degree followed by five years teaching English in Spain to be especially interesting. I have no particular hobbies, unless walking and being a Hispanophile count, and I'm not particularly well-read.

"If you are interested in people you are probably interesting yourself," he said, raising his eyebrows. He picked up the pipe, put it in his mouth, and lit it. He puffed on it a few times, creating a huge cloud of smoke that drew a glance of disapproval from Juanma, before tapping it on the side of the ashtray and putting it into his pocket, along with the three lighters, the penknife and the metal receptacle that resembled a snuff box.

"Are you going?"

"No, merely lowering my defences, ha, ha." His laugh was deep and merry, more like that of an older man.

"How old are you, Antonio?"

"Thirty-three. The age of Christ, as they say."

"And what do you work in, when you work?"

"I am an electrician, or rather, almost an electrician. I never finished my studies. When I am well I work with my brother."

"You seem well enough to me."

"But not to him, and not to my current doctor. I went to see her last week and after a very short conversation she gave me a sick note for another six months, and a prescription, of course."

"Why don't you just help your brother out a bit and see how it goes? It can't be good for you, sitting around in bars all day. Too much time to think."

"Maybe. Last week I signed up for karate classes. I begin tomorrow evening."

"That's good. Did you choose karate for any particular reason?"

"I like the clothes. I considered judo, but the human contact is excessive. I'm not aggressive in the least, but I think the physical exercise will be good for me."

"And you might meet some interesting people."

"I might."

"I usually go for walks at the weekend. You could come on one, if you fancy it."

"Where do you go?"

"I normally get the bus to Algezares or the Fuensanta sanctuary and walk up the hill from there. I get an early bus in summer and just walk for a couple of hours."

"On Saturday I would like to come. We could go in my car." He took one of three pens from his top jacket pocket and a block of post-it notes from an inside pocket. "Here is my mobile number."

I keyed the number into my phone and rang it. He stopped the call and recorded my name.

"Whereabouts do you live?" I asked him.

"In the Barrio del Carmen."

"Me too. On Mateos Street."

"I live on Goya Street."

"Ah, we are almost neighbours then," I said, recognising the name of a similarly narrow street to mine with the usual five storey blocks of flats on either side. "Do you live alone?"

"No, with my parents. That's why I spend so much time out of the flat."

"Do you not get on?"

"Oh, we get on all right, but they're old and don't understand my condition. My father says that nobody had time to be depressed when he was young... and things like that."

"We could meet in the Mesón de Juan at seven o'clock on Saturday morning," I said, referring to a friendly bar on a main street close to both our flats. I expected him to remark that seven o'clock was very early, but he merely nodded.

"I will be there at seven, Adam."

"Tomorrow night I help out in a friend's bar in the tascas. Come along if you like. It won't be busy."

"Where is it?"

I described the location of the nameless bar. "I think Dominic might be coming along tomorrow too."

"Dominic? The Dominic who comes in here?"

"Yes."

"I will see you on Saturday at seven," he said, his expression giving nothing away. "Now I must go home." He collected the few items that still remained on the bar and popped the rose into his top pocket.

"Wear some comfortable shoes on Saturday," I said.

"I will dress accordingly."

"And good luck with the karate tomorrow."

"Thank you."

He smiled, shook my hand, and left. I left shortly afterwards, feeling happy to have met such a singular character who didn't seem so odd after all.

3

Thursday nights in Jed's bar are very busy during term time as it is the traditional students' night out and many of them, both native and foreign, go to the tascas in search of cheap drinks. August, on the other hand, is a dead month in Murcia, but towards the end of it things begin to pick up. I opened the bar at seven, switched on the air conditioning, put on some music, poured myself a small draught beer, and waited.

There are six small, high tables in the bar, each with four stools, and by half past eight only one table was occupied, by a young Spanish couple, saying little and drinking less. At ten to nine the glass door opened and Dominic entered. He walked silently up to the narrow bar at the end of the room, his hands tucked into his denim jacket pockets, and perched himself on one of the three stools in front of the bar.

"Hello, Adam."

"I'm glad you could come."

"So this is a tascas bar," he said, looking around him as if he were in a cathedral.

"Come on, you must have been in the tascas before."

"Only to the Boca del Lobo," he said, referring to a heavy rock bar which played astonishingly loud music and served anyone who looked over fourteen.

"How's your week been?" I asked.

"I was very poorly at work on Monday. I should have gone home when you did. I never learn." He shook his head, tutted, and took a cigarette packet out of his jacket pocket and placed it on the bar.

"What would you like to drink? The first one's on me."

"Just a beer please."

"Large or small? It's draught, though there are bottles too."

"What do tascas people usually drink?"

"In this bar large ones, pints."

"A pint for me then. I must blend in," he said with a wink. He watched the ice-cold glass that I produced from the freezer fill with widening eyes.

I was laughing at his mock theatricals when Rob, a veteran Scottish language teacher, came in. We exchanged a few words in English while I poured the drinks which he then took over to a table to join his girlfriend.

"Mother of God, does one have to speak English here too?" Dominic said.

"Not unless you want to. When the students arrive next month there'll be plenty of Spanish people in here."

"Girls?"

"Lots."

"So I have until then to become a tascas person."

"What's your idea of a tascas person? I mean, they're just people who work or study like everybody else, just like in Infante."

"Do you remember the pub we walked into and straight out of on Sunday night?"

"Yes," I said, remembering it vividly.

"*That* is Infante. That is where I've been going since I was sixteen or seventeen. Half of my life, Adam, among those crazy, ignorant people."

"The Coyote seems like a fairly normal bar, and La Bomba is a rock bar."

"La Bomba is not an Infante bar. Troco chose the wrong place. The Coyote is a little decaffeinated, it's true, but I think if I'm to become a more cultivated person I should begin to spend time in the tascas," he said, quite seriously.

"One becomes cultivated, I should think, by reading books and, I don't know, visiting theatres and museums, rather than going to a certain kind of bar," I said.

"I've never read a book, Adam, unless you count car manuals." He scratched his nose and looked down at the bar, before drinking a third of his pint. "But," he went on, sitting erect, tapping his foot and wagging his finger alongside his head, "I'll try to relax and meet some people here."

"I'll introduce you to anyone I know who comes in."

"Good! Another pint, please."

"Aren't you going to...," I began, but the first glass was soon empty.

"Now I feel better. That's my first drink since Sunday. How much beer is in a pint?"

"They're half litres really."

"Easier to drink from these large glasses," he said, already making inroads into his second one.

Just then two rather unalluring young Englishwomen came in and sat at the table nearest to the door. I went over to serve them and when I returned to pour the beers I told Dominic that they didn't speak much Spanish, but that I'd be happy to introduce him.

"Well, Adam, if they don't speak Spanish perhaps it would be difficult," he said, moving his head from side to side and screwing up his face into a mask of comic deliberation.

"The... the larger one is very cultured."

"Let's see who else comes in."

I spent a while chatting to the girls at their table and when I returned, Dominic's glass was empty. I made him wait while I served a group of three placid young Spanish men who always came on Thursdays and always drank three pints each. I'd just poured Dominic another cold pint when Jed arrived. I was glad that the bar wasn't too empty because I knew he'd had a disturbingly quiet summer.

"How's it going, Adam?" he said, staying on the other side of the bar and pointing to the beer pump.

"Not too bad." I took a small glass from the shelf and poured him a beer. Jed was a big, tall, jovial man from near New York who had flunked out of college and worked as a waiter and barman for a few years before trying his luck in Spain. He was about Dominic's age, but I wondered what else they might have in common.

"Jed, this is Dominic, a friend of mine. He doesn't speak English," I said.

"Hola, Dominic. I'm glad you could come to my little bar," he said in his correct, heavily-accented Spanish. They shook hands and I saw that Dominic's eyes were regaining their Sunday sparkle.

"Pleased to meet you, Jed. This is the first time I've been to a tascas bar."

"Oh, are you from out of town?"

"No, I'm Murcian to the core, but I'm an Infante man."

"Infante? So you live across the river?" Jed said, apparently as ignorant of that element of Murcian nightlife as I had been until the previous Sunday.

"No, I live in San Andrés."

"Dominic means that he's always frequented the pubs over there," I said.

"Right," said Jed, a big smile masking a perplexity that was about to increase considerably.

"The Infante pubs, Jed," Dominic began, leaning right over towards him on the adjacent bar stool, "are where all the ignorant, uneducated people go. The music is loud and bad, the people drink too much and take drugs, and it's no place for a man of my age. From now on I will begin to come here and to other tascas and meet more cultured people, like you and Adam."

"Adam maybe, but there's not a lot of culture in here," Jed said, tapping his head and shooting a glance in my direction.

"And more cultured girls," Dominic went on before I could chip in. "The Infante girls wear too much make up, dress badly, talk worse, and have no moral values."

"Sounds good to me," said Jed, who until he met his rather severe wife Marisol had, as he put it, 'shagged anything that moved'.

"Here," Dominic said with a sweep of the hand, "I can already see that there is a higher class of person. Adam!" he turned to me and almost caught me with my head in my hands. "What books do you think I should read?"

"Well, er, I don't know. I suppose you could start with Don Quixote," I said, observing Jed's saucer-like eyes over Dominic's hunched shoulders.

"Of course, The Quixote!" He slapped his leg. "My mother has a copy. I will begin it tonight." He swung round to face Jed, who straightened his face just in time. "I'm also learning to play the drums, with Pedrín."

"The drums, that's great. I play the guitar a little."

"Good. We can form a group. At present my drum kit is in Pedrín's studio, but I can bring it here, tomorrow if you like."

"I'm afraid I don't have a music licence," he said, motioning me to turn the stereo down a little. "Who's Pedrín?"

"Pedrín… Adam, another pint please… Pedrín is one of the best drummers in Spain, if not the world. He plays with the Marañones who are very famous all over Spain."

"I've heard of them," Jed said.

"I will bring Pedrín here tomorrow. He always has words of advice for musicians."

"Yes do that, although it's always pretty packed on Fridays." He finished his glass of beer. "Well friends, I must be getting home now. I only came in to say hello. Pleased to meet you, Dominic."

"Pleased to meet *you*, Jed. I'll be coming here a lot from now on." He grasped Jed's hand and shook it hard, an intense, not to say maniacal, smile on his face.

I left Dominic drumming on the bar and went to attend to the other customers. I saw Jed slip into a bar across the street and, sure enough, heard the bleep of a text message about a minute later.

'Where did you find THAT fruitcake?' it read, much as I had expected. When I headed back to the bar I crossed paths with Dominic who was making a beeline for a table of three Spanish girls who had just arrived. I observed him as I rinsed out some glasses behind the bar and was relieved to see that he wasn't making an altogether bad impression. They were all laughing at whatever he was saying and when he swung round and headed back, the glances they exchanged were ones of surprise rather than consternation.

"Two JBs with coke and a small beer for the girls," he said, waiting poised to deliver the drinks.

"Er, I'd better take them over, Dominic."

"What? Oh, right, of course." He returned to his stool and resumed his finger and thumb drumming. "Nice girls," he said when I came back to the bar.

"Yes, I haven't seen them before."

"They look cultured. Do you think I should speak to them some more?"

"I would just let them settle in, if I were you. Perhaps have another word before you leave, or before they leave," I said, guessing that Dominic was likely to be my last customer of the night.

"Of course, patience. In Infante one must keep up the conversation or they forget who you are. Look!" he said, giving me a start. "Two more nice girls have arrived."

Before his foot hit the floor I was round the bar and off to attend to them. This wasn't lost on my friend as when I returned to pour their beers he wore a chastised look.

"I'm too impulsive, Adam. It's the fault of the uncultured people I've been mixing with all these years."

"Well, I'm no expert as far as women are concerned, but I believe it's best to be less direct, especially when they're sober. When's your next drumming class?" I asked, hoping to take his mind off the female clientele.

"Drumming class? Oh, I'll ring Pedrín soon."

"You have to stick at things, you know. With the money you probably spent on Sunday you could have had a couple of classes."

"Or three, or four," he said, looking at his glass and then at me like a repentant schoolboy. "I'll ring him at home now."

This he did and arranged to pick him up at eight o'clock on the following evening. He told me that the warehouse containing the rehearsal rooms lay about four kilometres outside Murcia, so I deduced that I'd done the drummer a double favour by securing him some beer money and conveyance to his no doubt precious drum kit. I later found that I'd been wrong about this second point as he cycled out there most days.

As Dominic was nearing the bottom of his fourth pint – a dangerous one, in my case at least – I decided to keep the pressure on.

"You'd better not drink much more if you're going to start Don Quixote tonight and be fit for work tomorrow," I said with what I hoped was a brotherly, even slightly paternal, smile.

"Yes, you're right," he said, slapping the bar. "As soon as I've started The Quixote I'll be able to talk about it. That will be useful when chatting to cultured girls."

I was going to tell him not to count on them having read it, but thought it might be better than his usual chat up lines, whatever they were. Beginning to feel quite schoolmasterly, I got back to the drums. "How many drum classes have you had so far, Dominic?"

"Oh, about ten, I think."

"Last night Pedrín told me you showed great promise."

"You saw him?"

"I called in at La Bomba, hoping to see you."

"Ach, had I not been so stupid and immature on Sunday I could have been there," he said, slapping his forehead.

Struggling to suppress a laugh, I pointed out a simple fact. "If you arranged to have classes with Pedrín on Tuesdays, Thursdays and Saturdays, for example, you would be sure of seeing him and could then go on to La Bomba with him afterwards for a drink."

"Yes, or I could bring him here, *and* he'd be able to pay for his own. Adam, you're a good friend and give good advice." He leant over the bar and patted my shoulder. "Nobody else gives me advice, except my mother. Just a small beer to finish with, please."

When I'd poured him the beer and gone to clear a couple of tables I remembered my other new friend, Antonio. I decided to plan another activity for Saturday.

"Dominic, when you meet Pedrín tomorrow why don't you arrange another class for about twelve o'clock on Saturday?"

"I could, but why?"

"Well, early on Saturday morning I'm going for a walk up around Fuensanta with a friend of mine. We're going in his car and I thought we could pop round and see you play the drums afterwards, if that's all right with you and Pedrín, and if you tell me how to get there."

"Of course, that would be great. Give me a sheet of paper and a pen, please." He made a rapid sketch. "Here it is, on the road to Santomera, past these warehouses and here on the right."

"Thanks, that's pretty clear. We could get there by twelve easily, or a bit later if you prefer to start the class without us."

"I'll let you know. Have you saved my number on your mobile?"

"Yes."

"Ring me now," he said, whipping his phone out of his jacket pocket and putting it to his ear. I did as requested and he quickly stored the number. "Who is this sporty friend of yours? Another Englishman?"

"No, a Murcian. Antonio, he's called. You know him by sight. He, er, well, he tends to arrange a lot of things on the bar when he's having a drink."

"What? That crazy man of the hill! You're joking?"

"No, I've been chatting to him and he seems perfectly normal. He's keen on karate, and walking... and music, I expect."

"No, Adam, no, no, no." He shook his head repeatedly. "You cannot take him to Pedrín's studio. He will... he will start to rearrange everything, or worse."

"I don't think so. He's a quiet, friendly guy."

"Many lunatics are quiet." His head was now still, but he had begun to wag his finger at me. "My great uncle Tomás was quiet, but ended up in the asylum all the same. How did you get to know him?"

"I just walked over and started talking to him. You should have tried it, instead of passing judgement straight away," I said, getting quite annoyed that Dominic of all people should dismiss a person I found, quite frankly, at least as sane as himself.

"All right, Adam, all right. Perhaps you're right, but please don't bring him to my drum classes just yet."

"Fair enough. It's Pedrín's place, after all."

"I shall go home now and read a few pages of The Quixote."

"You do that," I said, happy that we seemed to be reconciled. "I've read it in English and perhaps I'll have a go at it in Spanish too."

"Yes. I'll see you soon." He looked at me sadly. "Be careful with that crazy man."

"I will, but you'll see that I'm right."

4

When I arrived at Juan's almost empty bar at five past seven on Saturday morning I ordered a coffee with milk and asked him if anyone had been looking for me.

"Yes Adam, he's in the bathroom now," Juan said, an amused look on his face. Juan was a strong, sober man of about fifty and had become almost like an uncle to me in the year and a half that I'd known him. "He's been here since half past six," he added.

"In the bathroom?"

"No, at the bar drinking coffee and brandy." He pointed to a half-empty brandy glass surrounded by a ring of lighters. "Are you not walking this morning?"

"Yes."

"Here he comes."

I turned to see Antonio emerging from the bathroom wearing a martial arts jacket complete with matching white belt. As he approached I was relieved to see that he wore trousers underneath and shoes on his feet.

"Good morning, Adam," he said, a placid smile on his face. My last words to Dominic on Thursday night flashed before my mind's eye.

"Good morning, I see you've started your karate classes."

"Yes, I found the first class very enjoyable." He took a tiny sip of brandy. "But don't worry, I have a more suitable jacket in the car, and also a pair of trainers."

"Right. The jacket looks good," I said, determined to let Juan see that I was not fazed by my friend's eccentricity. Juan ought to know Antonio, him being a close neighbour of the bar, but any fact-finding enquiries would have to wait.

He looked down and adjusted the belt. "Yes, that's why I put it on this morning. My yellow belt, when I obtain it, will give the outfit a touch of colour."

"It's a green belt after that, isn't it?"

"Oh, I think I'll stick with yellow. It's a nice colour and I don't aspire to great things." He pushed the brandy away, asked Juan for a glass of water, and lit a cigarette.

August was over at last and the cool morning breeze promised a change in the weather, though I knew there'd be many hot days still to come. We got into Antonio's red, battle-scarred Seat Ibiza and he drove us slowly out of the city, through the village of Algezares and up towards the sanctuary. I suggested that we continue up the hill to a café and parking area from where we would be well-positioned for a walk that I suspected was not going to be a long one.

"That's fine by me, Adam," he said as he eased the car up the narrow, tree-lined road.

When we arrived we got out of the car and he filled his lungs with the fresh mountain air, before changing his jacket and putting on his trainers.

"It's a long time since I was last up here," he said, looking around him. "Smell the air, listen to the birds." He put on his sunglasses and lit a cigarette.

"It's better than pubs, anyway." I tightened my boot laces and put on my small rucksack containing two large bottles of water. "How far do you want to walk?"

"Oh, not so far." He looked at my brown legs. "But don't let me stop you from doing your usual walk. When I tire I will return to this nice café and take some refreshments."

In his black jeans I didn't think it would be long before he felt the heat of the unavoidable climb up the mountainside. After walking back along the narrow, twisting road for ten minutes I signalled a path heading off into the trees.

"This path takes us right to the top of the hill, but it's very steep."

"Lead on, Adam. I will follow."

I set off up the path a little more slowly than usual and after a few minutes I was pleased to hear his footfalls close behind me. I upped the pace for a while and when I stopped to take off my light jacket he did likewise and tied his around his waist. His black shirt looked incongruous up there amidst the pine trees and I was surprised to hear his untroubled breathing and see no sweat patches under his arms.

"Would you like some water?" I asked.

"When we get to the top."

And get to the top he did, still right behind me after a forty minutes slog that left me dripping with sweat. From the unpaved track onto which we emerged there was a good view down the mountainside towards the coast and after wiping a bead of sweat from his temple he put on his jacket, took a sip of water from the bottle I offered him without clamping his lips to the neck, and lit a cigarette.

"You're fitter than I thought you'd be," I said, towelling my hair with a spare t-shirt after I'd downed half a bottle of water.

"Ah," he said with a shrug.

"Do you walk much?"

"Around the city, yes, many kilometres. Where to now?"

"Now we can follow this track along here for a while. It'll take us back down and around to the café. No more sweating for me, unless that sun gets really hot."

"Don't worry about your sweating. It's genetic."

"Genetic?"

"Yes, or hereditary. You're from the cold north, whereas my ancestors worked in the fields down there for countless generations; until this one, in fact. Ha, ha, come on, or we'll catch a chill."

He led the way down the track with great loping strides and only when we reached the tarmac road back to the café did he begin to show signs of fatigue.

"Phew, I'm ready for something to eat," he said after slumping down into a plastic chair and loosening his shoelaces.

We ordered small baguette sandwiches with red wine and lemonade and set about restoring the tissues, as Wodehouse used to say. What a pleasant morning it was turning out to be, and how foolish I thought Dominic for dismissing Antonio as an irretrievable crackpot! One just has to know how to treat people and they usually respond well, I thought at a quarter past eleven that fine morning, feeling contented beneath the shade of the trees.

By a quarter to twelve I wasn't feeling so sure of myself. After demolishing the bottle of strong red wine, normally only used to give a little taste to the lemonade, he had ordered a coffee and large brandy and changed back into his karate jacket. The more people arrived to occupy the other tables, the more animated he became. He was giving me a blow by blow account of his first karate class and I could see that a demonstration was fast approaching.

"I was the oldest person in the beginners' class, in fact the other seven students were teenagers and children. First of all the instructor told us a little about the philosophy of karate - that it's a martial art that trains us to be peaceful. This disappointed a couple of the teenage boys, but when he added that if conflict is unavoidable, one should be able to incapacitate one's opponent with a single blow, they became more cheerful again.

"To be honest, all his talk about the body, mind and spirit seemed to bore the younger students and they were pleased when he began to teach us the first moves." He stood up and I slid down a little in my chair. "First he made us stand with our fists like this. Then he moved forward and moved his arm like that and we copied him. Then he made us turn to one side and hit the air like this. Then we turned one more time and we all had to cry out HAAA!"

This attracted a considerable amount of attention from the other customers and even a little clapping which Antonio acknowledged with a stiff bow before sitting down again.

"We performed those moves, and some more, many times. He says that I show promise, despite my age." He drank some brandy and lit a cigarette. "I have my second class next Thursday."

"Did the first lesson not make you stiff?" I asked, keen to keep him in his chair.

"A little, but we also did some stretching." He began to rise, but saw my discomfiture and lowered himself back into the chair. "Do my demonstrations embarrass you, Adam?"

"A bit, with all these people around."

"Have a drink and try to relax. Don't worry so much about what other people think."

I ordered a beer and found that just holding the bottle made me feel a little less uptight. If I wanted to spend time with Antonio, who made a refreshing change from my usual cronies, I'd have to learn to chill out a bit.

"Do you like Chinese food?" he asked me.

"I don't mind it."

"Then I'll invite you to lunch at my favourite Chinese restaurant."

"Ok, but you don't have to pay for me."

"Oh yes, I insist. My monthly payment will be in the bank."

"Let's go halves."

"No. In fact, both my monthly payments will be in the bank by now."

"You get two?"

"Yes, one because of my condition and the other, well, I don't know, but I receive almost 130,000 pesetas each month." He smiled and spread his hands, palms up.

"That's not bad," I said, conscious of the fact that an unskilled worker would be unlikely to earn more. "I suppose you give some to your parents for board."

"A little, yes, but now you see how I'm able to spend most of my time in the street," by which he meant in bars and pubs rather than on the street itself.

"Have you thought about getting your own place? Then you wouldn't need to be out all the time."

"Hmm, the problem is that I'm not sure how long the payments will last."

"Perhaps you'll be fit to go back to work with your brother soon."

He breathed in through his teeth and beckoned the waiter. "My brother reacts far worse than you to my little eccentricities... A beer please and one for my friend... During the course of a day with him I'm certain to do something to displease him at least once or twice. Then he tells me that he has no more work for me." He drained his brandy glass and lit a cigarette.

"But can you not stop doing the... eccentric things that you do. I mean, I don't mind in the least, but if it bothers your brother..."

"No!" he snapped, his face clouding and his smile returning in the space of a few seconds. "No, I am as I am and cannot change for his convenience. People think me strange, but never stop to look at themselves. My brother works inhuman hours and only thinks about money. For him that's normal, so I don't tell him to stop doing it. The zhajiangmian is very good."

"The what?"

"Zhajiangmian is a dish of noodles and sauce that my Chinese friends prepare very well. Are you hungry?"

"I will be soon, but I'd like to have a shower first."

"Of course. We'll stop at your flat before we go." He drank most of his beer and stood up. "I'll bring the car."

By the time I'd finished my beer – I was, and am, still unable to get out the English habit of never leaving a drop – the car was idling a yard from the table, rather closer than the people seated nearby would have liked. When I'd got into the car I heard the words, 'he's crazy or drunk' coming from their direction and Antonio heard them too.

"Crazy, sane, drunk, sober. What's the difference?" he said as he pulled slowly away.

"Do you want to come up?" I said when he had stopped on the narrow street outside my flat.

"Some other time. I'll wait here."

"You'll have to go around the block if any cars come. I'll be as quick as I can."

I rode the lift up to my fourth floor flat, a large one with only myself in residence as the landlord had left it up to me to find co-tenants and after a couple of bad experiences I'd decided to pay all of the modest rent myself. Ten minutes later I rode back down again, much refreshed, and saw about ten minutes' worth of cars lined up behind Antonio's Ibiza, most of them tooting their horns and one irate giant making his way towards the front of the queue with murder in his eyes.

"Go!" I said when I'd dropped into the seat.

"Yes," he drawled as he accelerated away. "That man was filling my mirror with hatred." He turned onto Alameda Capuchinos, the shopping street leading to the Infante strip, and pulled into a small parking zone on the left.

"You could have driven around the block," I said, as calmly as I could.

"I could, but it was amusing to observe the reaction of those people, all in such a hurry."

"That guy was furious."

"Yes, I would have pulled away had you not arrived. The restaurant is just a little way down the street."

Needless to say, Antonio wore his new karate jacket to the large, windowless Chinese restaurant which was about a third full when we arrived at half past two. Despite its proximity to my flat I had never eaten there, not being especially partial to oriental cuisine or to dining alone. Until recently I had simply lived in the Barrio del Carmen and crossed the bridge to the city centre to do everything bar shopping for the little food that I kept in the flat.

Antonio led me to 'his' table, near to the bar and the kitchen doors, the better to be closer to his friends, May and June, the daughters of the house. They were both pretty, petite girls in their early-twenties and their businesslike, inscrutable faces lit up every time my friend addressed them, which was often.

May complemented him on his karate jacket and he offered to show her what he had learnt so far.

"Later," she said, spinning her index finger to denote the passage of time as the Spanish do. "When it's quiet, you can show me. Now you must eat."

"May, this is my good friend Adam. He's English."

"Hello," she said, her smile not quite as open as the ones she bestowed on him.

"It's curious that your names are also names in English," I said, keen to make some kind of mark, however pedantic.

"Ha, they're our English names chosen for us by our father," she said, tilting her head in the direction of the kitchen. "He thought they would be easier for the customers to pronounce."

"Yes, but in English your name is pronounced 'may' rather than 'mai'," I couldn't help saying.

"Whatever," she said with a shrug. "Will you start with zhajiangmian as usual, Antonio?"

"Yes dear. I recommend it, Adam."

"Ok, I'll have that too," I said, trying to replicate May's insouciant shrug.

We ate heartily and when Antonio handed June the empty red wine bottle as she passed by our table half way through the main course I put all thoughts of a long siesta out of my mind. I would keep up with my friend for a while and retire at some point during the evening. Jed would have to manage without me that night.

Antonio thought that a bottle of cava would go nicely with dessert and I thought so too.

"Is it wise to mix so much drink with your medication," my conscience forced me to say before I was past caring.

"I haven't taken my tablets today." He sipped his cava and raised his eyebrows, smiling mischievously.

What the hell, I thought. As long as I kept him on this side of the river my good name, such as it was, would be safe. It wasn't as if I was inciting him to do anything he wouldn't have done anyway. Nor was it me who ordered two glasses of baijiu, a kind of Chinese firewater, with coffee.

We had eaten and drunk more than we had spoken during the meal, but with the baijiu assisting our digestion – or burning up the food before it left our stomachs – Antonio became more loquacious.

"What do you think of this place, Adam?" he drawled.

"I like it. May and June are nice. They like you," I drawled back.

"Yes, because I am different."

"Vive la difference."

"Yes, the other customers just come here to fill their bellies, whereas I take an interest in them. There are four children. May and June have to work here, but their young brother and sister, Huan and Shu, are expected to go to university."

"That seems unfair."

"The law of life. May and June were fifteen and fourteen when they arrived in Spain about six years ago, so their education is not complete, although they now speak Spanish well. Their father has higher aspirations for the younger ones."

"And their mother?"

"She feels the same. She'll be in the kitchen too and will appear later to say hello, no doubt. I've spent many hours in this restaurant, not usually drinking as much as today, and find it very relaxing."

When most of the other diners had left, May left June to clear the remaining plates and came to our table.

"Now you must go home to rest, Antonio," she said, leaning on the back of the spare chair, her head not too far above ours.

"Take a seat, May," he said.

"No, from here I can watch over you. What's your name again?" she asked me.

"Adam."

"Adam, please don't let him go to those horrible bars down there. He'll drink more and I bet he hasn't taken his medication today. What do you do?"

"I teach English."

"Ah, my young brother and sister are learning English at the language school," she said, wistfully, I thought.

"*You* should learn English," Antonio said, suddenly serious, "and June too. Tell your father to give you some time off."

"He needs us here."

"Bah! Just a few hours. Tell him I want to speak to him."

"He's busy," she said, drifting away from the table and into the kitchen.

"Antonio, you are raising your voice," said June, who took her sister's place behind the chair. Slightly younger and even prettier than her sister, she also looked tougher. She cast a disapproving glass at our baijiu glasses.

"Why are you drinking that Chinese poison? At least have a nice, smooth brandy if you have to drink."

"June will make a demanding wife," said Antonio without taking his eyes off her.

"Yes, no husband of mine will spend the afternoon drinking in a restaurant."

I refrained from saying that he would probably spend most of them on the other side of the kitchen doors and instead asked her if she liked Murcia.

"What I see of it, yes. Go home to rest now, Antonio," she said as she too drifted away.

The back of the chair was only free for a short while before the as yet unseen mother took her place there. She looked about forty and a life spent indoors didn't appear to have diminished her good looks and cheerfulness too much. She spoke Spanish badly, but made herself understood.

"Antonio, you eat good?"

"A splendid meal, Señora Song, thank you."

"Yes, it was delicious," I chipped in.

"You Antonio friend?"

"Yes, I am."

"You take home now, please. Not go bars drink more," she said, wagging her finger at the object of her scolding.

"I'll try."

"No shot on house today, Antonio. You drink much already," she said before returning to the kitchen.

I was wondering if the father would be next to grace the chair back, but my only view of him was when he pushed the kitchen door ajar with the back of his hand and scowled in our general direction. The girls had got their looks from their mother.

"I just spotted the father. Does he not like you?"

"Oh, he's normally all right with me. May probably mentioned the English classes." He chuckled through a haze of cigarette smoke. "Another glass of baijiu?"

"Good God, no. It does seem to aid digestion though."

"It eats food, ha, ha. Shall we move on?"

"Home?"

"Ha, ha. May! June! We are leaving."

May appeared and brought us the bill which he paid before I could protest.

"Now that the restaurant is empty you can show me your karate moves, Antonio," she said, an impish smile on her face.

He slowly rose to his feet and shuffled into the aisle. He staggered first to one side and then to the other, causing May to fold her arms and shake her head. His head lolled forward and I was about to escort him back to the table when he suddenly snapped to attention and took up his position. He went through the moves just as well as he had done that morning, not forgetting the final 'HAAA!' which brought the rest of the family to the kitchen doors. He bowed gravely, I waved limply, and we left the restaurant.

"Where to now?" I asked as we headed back to the car.

"Shall we go to see your American friend?"

"He doesn't open for another three hours," I said, not quite truthfully as he would open at seven, but I was more determined than ever not to cross river.

"To the Coyote, then." He took out his keys.

"Can we not walk? It's only about 400 metres away."

"What if we want to move on somewhere else later?"

"It's 400 metres back here too."

"Very well, although later I may be too drunk to walk so far."

My memories of the rest of the afternoon are rather sketchy, but I remember that another karate demonstration took place in the Coyote, rewarded by drinks from a gleeful customer who couldn't stop laughing, rubbing his nose and making frequent trips to the bathroom. On the whole, though, I think we were fairly discreet and I noticed that Antonio only adorned his bar space with a rose bought from one of the Chinese ladies who did the rounds of the pubs.

"She's worse off than May and June," I remember commenting just before Dominic arrived and sat on a stool some way to my left. He nodded briefly before ordering a beer and talking to the pretty barmaid for as long as he could hold her attention, after which he appeared to become lost in reverie.

"Come and join us, Dominic," I said, to which he responded with an almost imperceptible shake of the head and a condolatory smile.

Shortly afterwards Antonio squeezed my arm and said he must be going. Before I had time to protest, he was gone and Dominic had moved his stool to my side. I recall the subsequent conversation as going something like this.

"Oh, Adam, what are you doing?"

"Just having a quiet drink with a friend," I said as clearly as I could.

"Adam, what a state you are in, and at this time of the afternoon! I hoped we could go to Jed's bar later, after my drumming class, but I see that the bad company that you keep has left you in a terrible state. I warned you about that crazy man, didn't I?"

"We've been for a long walk in the mountains and eaten a marvellous Chinese meal. Just had a little too much to drink, that's all."

"So you've been all over the place with him in that ridiculous judo jacket. Think about your reputation as a teacher."

"Karate jacket. I'll show you some moves," I said, preparing to stand.

"Please, stay still, Adam. I also have my reputation to consider. I planned for us to go to Pedrín's studio and then on to Jed's bar, but I can't let my maestro see you in this state. Did you read my text message?"

"Phone at home. I'll go home to rest now and meet you in La Bomba at about... nine," I said when I got my watch face into focus.

"I doubt it. I doubt it very much, and I had so wanted to discuss the first part of The Quixote with you."

"Have you finished the first part already? That's going some."

"Yes, all of the first chapter. Now, off you go and I hope to see you at nine."

I left, but I did not return.

5

I didn't enter another bar until the following Thursday and then only because I had to open Jed's. It wasn't that I was hungover or repentant after Saturday's outing – twelve hours' sleep ensured that I awoke on Sunday feeling only slightly below par – but the intensity of my encounters with both Antonio and Dominic made me decide to take a step back for a while.

Being a person whose friends and acquaintances could all be said to fall within the spectrum of normality, to have met just one of those singular individuals would have been more than enough to be going on with, but meeting both of them within the space of a few days left me feeling quite drained.

I was no writer either, apart from keeping a diary of sorts, so it wasn't as if I was on the lookout for material. Perhaps I should stay away from Infante, I thought, and carry on networking the English teaching scene in search of new customers. Private students can be a fickle lot and it's always wise to have candidates ready to plug the gaps when people drop out.

All this went through my mind as I stood behind the bar on Thursday night, watching and listening to the folk occupying five of the six tables. They talked about classes, cars, football and money, among other mundane things, and I wondered what my two new friends would be doing. By half past nine I wouldn't have minded if one of them had walked through the door and by half past ten I was sorry that neither of them had. Perhaps they didn't think I was worth a trip into the tascas to see. I wasn't especially interesting, after all.

"Adam, are you coming out tomorrow," said Richard, interrupting my reverie. Richard was a blond lad of twenty-three from Reading who was ever so keen to carry on where he'd left off after his first year's work in Murcia; meeting everybody who mattered in the language teaching scene and looking for a pretty, sensible, Spanish girlfriend.

"What's the plan?"

"Me, Geoff and Simon are going to grab some food at the Italian in the Santo Domingo square and then hit the tascas. We might go on to a disco later."

"Right, well, I'm not sure yet," I said, envisaging the pilgrimage from bar to bar and the struggle to get served in most of them.

"Well, we're meeting here at eight if you fancy it. Now that it's September it should be buzzing again"

"Ok, I might see you here."

At eight o'clock on the following evening I walked into La Bomba and found the length of the bar – all five or six yards of it – lined with people. This was as pleasing as it was unexpected and, as I couldn't see Dominic or Pedrín, I squeezed in between a slender middle-aged man with a quiff and an attractive girl with a very fetching short haircut.

"Picha, you missed a great concert on Wednesday," said Troco, raising his hand above the bar for me to clasp and exhaling jets of thick smoke through his nostrils. "Adam, this is Alberto, El Zorro (The Fox), one of the best guitarists in Murcia."

"In Spain, in Spain," the man said hoarsely before shaking my hand in the old-fashioned way.

"And…?" I began, looking at the girl because I didn't want her to feel left out.

"This is Carolina, my girl," Troco said. She nodded. "Carolina, this is Adam, the best English teacher in Murcia."

"In Spain," I said, hoping that El Zorro wouldn't take it the wrong way. He didn't take it either way, because his head was leaning back as he drained his long glass before plonking it down on the bar and lighting a cigarette. He was an aging rocker if ever I saw one; jet black hair, surely dyed, held back with gel to cover his thinning pate; black leather jacket, black shirt, blue jeans and pointy black boots. Oh, and long sideburns, of course.

"A JB with cola, Troco," he said, casting his eyes along the bar.

Troco's moll was playing with her phone, so despite El Zorro's – let's call him Alberto – lack of interest in me I decided to make conversation.

"What's the name of your group?"

"What? My group? Ah, my group. My real group is no more. My real group was Los Leones (The Lions). We revolutionised rock music in Murcia in the 70s, then my compadre – the best bass player in Murcia and one of the best in Spain – decided to meet a German girl and go off to live in Dusseldorf."

"I suppose he couldn't help that," I said, nodding to Troco, who was holding a bottle of beer and an opener like a bullfighter holds his banderillas before sticking them in the poor bull.

"Meeting her, no, but to go to *Germany*, for God's sake. What do they know about rock music in Germany?" he asked. I shrugged. "He stopped playing. Now he is a nobody." A long drink took the scowl off his face.

"Who do you play with now?"

"Pah, now I have a group that isn't worthy of a name, so I don't name it. We play in the village fiestas and at weddings and only this makes me go on." He rubbed his finger and thumb together.

"Do you play, or sing?"

"No, I can't play any instruments. I used to sing in the choir at school," I said, trying to inject a note of humour into proceedings.

"Hmm, and you are English, you say?"

"Yes, a teacher."

"I have *another* group, you see, which I am trying to get into some sort of shape. I have a young bass player and drummer, and also a young guitarist to accompany me, but they insist on playing mostly American blues songs. None of them sing. I can sing, but will not sing in English. I refuse to sing a song if I can't understand the words. It would be good if you could come to our rehearsal on Saturday. We meet at Luis the bass player's house in the country."

"I'd like that," I said, assuming that he wanted me to translate some songs, but happy to go along for the ride.

"I'll pick you up here at four o'clock."

"Right. I'll be here."

"But don't drink too much before we meet, please, like Chema, the so-called guitarist, sometimes does."

"Of course not. I'll have my wits about me," I said, tapping my head.

"Your wits and your voice."

"My voice?"

"Yes, you must not slur the words."

About to protest that singing blues songs was not on my list of achievements or aspirations, I was saved, or so I thought, by the arrival of Dominic.

"Alberto, Adam, how are things going?" he said, his eyes bright and clear. I was pleased that he had made for us after greeting most of the other customers fleetingly. "I see you have met El Zorro, Adam, a legend in Murcia."

"Yes, but Alberto is under the impression that I-"

"Adam here is going to rehearse with the group tomorrow," Alberto said.

"What do you play?" Dominic asked, puzzled.

"I don't play or si-"

"Adam is a singer. He can sing the blues in English."

"You didn't tell me that, you rascal!" Dominic said, slapping me on the back. "It's true that you have a nice voice. I'll come tomorrow to lend my support. I can play the drums if Lucky doesn't turn up."

"Lucky will turn up," said Alberto.

"Listen to me, both of you," I said, raising my hands to get their attention. "I'm not a singer. I don't know any blues songs. I'm not even a big fan of the blues."

"Ah, but it's in the blood," said Alberto.

"But I'm not even black."

"English blood. There have been some excellent English blues singers. John Mayall, Alexis Korner, Joe Cocker; all English, all white.

"Oh, Adam, you're too modest," said Dominic. "Have you sung with many groups?"

"None!"

"That's good," said Alberto. "He won't have picked up any bad habits. Troco! Take off that execrable Spanish rock music and please play the blues CD that I gave you."

The upbeat music soon came to an end and was replaced by a twanging guitar, mournful harmonica and a slow bass line.

"Muddy Waters," said Alberto, looking at me expectantly.

When Muddy began to sing *Louisiana Blues* I kept my lips firmly shut and signalled to Troco to open another beer for me.

"Sing," said Alberto.

"I don't know the words," I said.

"No, no, that song is too slow and too... too black for Adam to sing," said Dominic. "He prefers faster songs."

"Do I?"

"Yes, let's wait for a better one."

"Picha," said Troco to Alberto, "my customers will cut their wrists or leave if I play this music."

"Put on number seven, no, eight. Adam's going to sing."

Troco, intrigued by this idea, turned to the music system and a few seconds later somewhat jauntier tones could be heard, followed by the words, 'One bourbon, one scotch, and one beer'.

"This is John Lee Hooker, as you know, Adam," said Alberto. "Even I know what the chorus means."

"I've got that bit, but I don't know the rest of it."

"Make it up," said Dominic, busy finger-drumming on the bar. "We won't know the difference."

When the chorus came around for the fourth or fifth time I sang along, pronouncing each word in my best BBC accent. Seeing this have the desired effect, I improvised the rest of the song in a voice reminiscent of David Niven.

"Maybe not," said Alberto before draining his glass.

"Can I come along tomorrow anyway?" I asked him.

"Well..."

"Of course," said Dominic. "I'll pick you up here. I'm sure that Lucky will let me play the drums for a while."

Alberto, a.k.a. El Zorro, raised his eyes to the ceiling like a wounded fox before going to join a crony at the other end of the bar.

"Will he mind, now that he knows that I'm no singer?" I asked Dominic.

"It's not his house. Anyway, if we take a bottle of JB he will be more than happy."

"I've never seen a group rehearse before."

"Do you really sing so badly?"

I sang a few lines of the Led Zeppelin song which Troco had just put on, trying my best to imitate Robert Plant.

Dominic grimaced. "Yes, we'll take a bottle of JB."

"Shall we go to the Coyote for one in a while?" I said, relieved that my singing days were over.

"Yes, we could." His eyes narrowed. "Have you seen that crazy man again?"

"I haven't see Antonio since last Saturday, if that's who you mean."

"He may be there, dressed in his judo jacket, or in a ballet outfit." He shuddered. "I must keep you away from him, for your own good."

"Antonio is a nice guy and isn't crazy at all. He has his little eccentricities, but don't we all? Don't you?"

"Are you comparing me to *him*?"

"No, but, I mean, you're not a very conventional person either, are you?"

"You're comparing me to him." He swivelled round to face the bar. "Troco! Another beer, please."

"What I mean is this," I said into his left ear. "You're an effusive, impulsive person. You play the drums on the bar. You get in your car and drive to the beach and then drive straight back again. In short, you're a character. Antonio's a character too. You should at least give him a chance, get to know him."

Dominic's eyes stayed focussed on the row of bottles behind the bar. I was fed up of this nonsense and decided to take things a step further.

"Are you scared of him?"

"What? Ha, no judo outfit scares me. Even now with my one lung I could pick him up and throw-"

"I don't mean like that. I mean, are you scared to talk to him? Are you scared that you'll like him and end up being his friend, sitting at the bar with him in his karate jacket."

Dominic turned towards me. "Listen, Adam, I know from what others have told me that he sees a psychiatrist and takes a lot of medication. He is *officially* crazy and has the papers to prove it. I have not been to any kind of doctor since I recovered from my accident. I am just impulsive and… and creative."

"You're scared to meet him."

"Damn you and your English meddling. Finish your beer and we'll go to speak to him now. There are no decent girls here anyway."

After all that, Antonio wasn't in the Coyote.

"He was in yesterday afternoon for a while," said Juanma when I asked.

"In his judo outfit?" asked Dominic.

"No, dressed normally. Less stuff on the bar too."

Resolving to call him on Sunday, I asked Dominic how he was getting on with Don Quixote.

"I have reached the end of chapter four."

"That's good. Are you enjoying it?"

"The language is a little old-fashioned, but the story is good. He's just been knighted by the innkeeper. Don Quixote was crazier than your friend Antonio."

"But you like him?"

"So far, yes, but I wouldn't drink with him."

6

We took it easy that evening and at four o'clock the following afternoon I entered La Bomba carrying a bottle of JB whisky in a plastic bag. I put it on the bar next to Dominic's identical bottle.

"Leave yours in the car," I said.

"I will, but it won't stay there. These rehearsal sessions can become very long affairs. Have you eaten?"

"Yes."

"Good, let's go."

"Enjoy yourselves," said Troco, about to be left alone, "and bring the others back here afterwards."

Dominic drove us out of the city on the Santomera road before turning left onto a lane through flat fields forming part of *La Huerta*, or orchard, of Murcia. We passed several houses – some imposing, most humble – before arriving at a big, austere bungalow with two cars and three Harley Davidson motorbikes parked on the dusty driveway.

"Nice bikes." I said as we approached the house.

"Luis, Chema and Lucky all decided they had to buy one. I think Lucky's was the first."

"They must have cost a bit."

"They're only Sportsters, the cheapest model," Dominic said with a dismissive wave of the hand.

The boys weren't yet in action when we walked into the huge living room and I put the whisky bottle on a trestle table next to a half-empty one, two large bottles of coke and a plastic bucket of ice. Introductions were made and they all seemed friendly, except Alberto, who was brooding and smoking on the tatty sofa.

Luis, the owner of the house which had started life as an unsuccessful bar and restaurant, was in his early-thirties, slightly-built and with longish, receding hair. He shook my hand and smiled, but said little and soon began to tune up his bass guitar. Chema, about the same age, was a muscular, short-haired chap with a cheeky smile, and his clumsy way of moving made me doubt that he was much of a guitarist.

Lucky hadn't been too lucky as regards physical beauty. He was one of those gawky young men whose maker had added to his general ugliness an unfair gum to teeth ratio, the gums coming out the easy winners over his irregular ivories. He was friendly enough, in a dreamy sort of way, and had no objection to Dominic having a bash on his drums before they started the rehearsal proper.

"Adam, please fix me a JB and coke," he said to me before dashing over to the drum kit. Alberto cursed and covered his ears before Dominic had even picked up the sticks, but the steady beat that he produced didn't sound too bad to me. Luis was by that time picking out a straightforward bass line and Dominic watched his fingers intensely as he strove to provide suitable accompaniment.

"I thought Pedrín had given him some classes," said Alberto from the sofa, shaking his head.

"He's not doing too badly," said Lucky.

"He will never be a musician," said the older man.

Chema, perhaps in an act of solidarity with the aspiring drummer, picked up his splendid guitar – a Gretsch, I saw – and plugged it in. He strummed a few chords to get Luis playing what he wanted, before launching into an extended solo that took my breath away. Dominic's face was a joy to watch as he strove to keep the beat steady and, when Chema finally wound up his virtuoso improvisation, he finished with what even I could tell was a rather inept flourish. He tossed the drumsticks into the air, dropped one, picked it up, and stayed rooted to the stool.

"That's enough fooling around," said Alberto, pushing himself to his feet. "Let's get down to business."

Lucky ambled over to the drums and Dominic reluctantly ceded his place. Alberto plugged in his scruffy blue Fender and tuned it up.

"Take a break for now, Chema, until I get these two doing what I want," he said.

Chema placed his guitar carefully onto its stand and made himself a drink, not seeming to mind his exclusion.

"As we have no singer yet for the blues songs you want to play," Alberto said, catching my eye for the first time since I'd arrived, "we'll go through some of my songs first."

Lucky puffed out his cheeks on hearing this, but Luis didn't demur, standing as he was right in front of Alberto.

"Uno, dos, tres, cuatro," began the old rocker, before launching into an adroit opening riff that the others followed with ease. Lucky's firm beat put Dominic's efforts into context and Luis seemed to be playing a very competent bass line. It sounded great to me until Alberto began to sing.

I already knew he was a heavy smoker, but his croaky voice could have been used as a before and after ad for aspiring vocalists. He made Bob Dylan sound like an angel. Tom Waits with a sore throat sprang to mind. Still, the music was good, or was it? Towards the end of the song – a rock ditty about whisky and women, for a change – I realised that he was playing the same short solo over and over again.

They moved straight onto the second song – about a woman who'd left him – and I heard that riff, or something very similar, pop up again. I stole a glance at Chema, but his mind appeared to be elsewhere. Dominic was tapping his foot and looking out of the window. Lucky kept the beat but looked bored. Luis was deep in concentration and I soon saw why.

"Stop, stop," croaked Alberto, waving his skinny arms in the air. "Luis, what the fuck was that? Don't try fancy stuff, because you can't do it. My God, this is what comes of playing with amateurs."

I was taken aback by this tirade, but Luis just smirked and tweaked a couple of strings. Lucky threw his sticks in the air and caught them, while Chema wandered outside for some air. Dominic poured himself another whisky and I joined him at the drinks table.

"He seems annoyed," I whispered.

"Ha, don't pay any attention to El Zorro. He's always like that. He thinks he's the great pro and they all humour him. A couple more whiskies and he might sit down and let them get on with it."

After four or five more uninspiring Spanish rock songs, all penned by Alberto in his younger days, they took a drinks break. Dominic seized the opportunity to return to the drums. Chema responded to his request to join him and was soon playing a slow blues, pausing occasionally to give Dominic a few pointers. After a few minutes he took his place at the drum kit and showed him how it was done, before returning to his guitar. He was very patient with my friend, but the tutorial didn't last long.

"Get off those drums, Dominic, you're giving me a headache. You stay there, Chema, and we'll go through some of those blues songs," said Alberto.

Chema took the lead this time and Alberto was relegated to playing rhythm guitar with a bored look on his face. They sounded great and I regretted being unable to help them with the vocals. I saw there was little whisky left by this time and I suggested to Dominic that I fetch the other bottle from the car.

"No, no, leave it," he said, leaning towards me on the sofa. "Alberto is being especially obnoxious today and if he wants more he can go and get it himself. That way he'll give us a break."

"I don't know why they put up with him. They don't need him, after all. It's Luis's house and Chema's a brilliant guitarist."

"Ah, but they do need him."

"Why?"

"Because without him they would never get organised. Luis and Chema would have got so drunk last night that they'd have done nothing today. They're both lorry drivers and normally get back to Murcia on Friday evening. Then they go out and... well, you can imagine. Also, Alberto has taught Luis a lot over the years so he feels grateful. Alberto also has the contacts to arrange gigs. Without him they will never play in public."

"But what about Chema? Where does he fit in?"

"He's Luis's best friend. He's very talented, but he doesn't care about playing concerts. He's also a little crazy."

"Like Antonio?"

"No, not that kind of crazy. More like my kind of crazy. I mean, not really crazy at all, just impulsive. He gets very drunk and has ridden his bike into ditches twice now. His record in the lorry is not good either, though that's due to recklessness rather than drunkenness. He has a lovely girlfriend in Caravaca and rarely sees her."

"I see."

"Oh, he'll grow up and settle down one day," he said, like a wise old man lamenting the youth of today. "Give me your glass. There's hardly any whisky left."

Soon after Dominic had made our drinks the group took a break and made for the refreshments table.

"I shit myself on the whore mother," said Alberto when he saw the empty JB bottle. "Who's going to get some more whisky?"

"I brought the first bottle," said Lucky.

"I bought the coke and ice," said Luis.

"I have no money," said Chema, winking at me.

"Amateur musicians and amateur drinkers, the lot of you," said Alberto without a trace of mirth.

"There's a bar just up the road," said Luis.

"I know, damn it, I've been enough times. You know what? I've had enough of this messing about for today." Without another word he put his guitar and lead into their case and left the house.

When his car accelerated away down the lane Dominic jumped to his feet, rubbed his hands together and went to fetch the whisky from his car. He left it on the table before picking up his glass and making straight for the drums, where he resumed his usual beat. After a drink and a smoke Luis and Chema joined him and Dominic spent a heavenly half hour before handing the drumsticks to Lucky.

Chema switched on the microphone and sang a Spanish rock song not at all badly.

"Why don't you sing in the group?" I asked him when the song was over.

"What? And listen to that old bastard's complaints all the time. No thanks."

Dominic unclipped the microphone from the stand and began to improvise a blues, in Spanish, of course.

"*El Zorro said we could not play,*" he wailed, the others picking up the tune.

"With a crowd like you I will not stay,
 A pro like me can't fall so low,
 I'm just too good, I've got to go,
 This old time rocker's got the superiority blues."

That's more an approximation than a translation, but he went on for quite a while in the same vein until he collapsed on the sofa in mock exhaustion. I was impressed by his spontaneous composition and told him so.

"Oh, it's nothing. I did something similar in La Bomba once with many people there and Pedrín on the drums. I got a lot of applause." He lit a cigarette and looked dreamily at the ceiling.

"You should work on that, and on the drums too. If you stick at it you could achieve something. I wish I was more musical," I said, quite sincerely, because at that time I didn't have any creative outlet at all, not even my scribblings.

"We'll go to La Bomba in a while and I'll arrange my next class with Pedrín."

And that's what we did. After a raucous entrance into the local bar for beer, food and coffee all five of us made our way to the only rock bar in Infante, much to Troco's delight.

The rest of the night was a bit of a blur, but while I enjoyed myself with my new pals I wondered if Antonio would be sitting alone at the bar in the Coyote. As I wandered back past the Chinese restaurant towards my flat well after midnight I promised myself that I would call him the following afternoon.

7

I didn't need to call him because at half past eleven the next morning he rang my doorbell. I was going to turn over and ignore its insistent tones, but when I realised that it wasn't the sound of the downstairs buzzer I thought I'd better get up and see which of the neighbours was calling. I peered round the door and there he was, dressed in a dark suit and flowery tie.

"Good morning, Adam. I hope I didn't wake you," he said, his neatly parted hair shining in the dim light.

"No, no, I was just getting up. How did you get in?"

"I didn't know your number, so I pressed the buttons until one of your neighbours let me in."

"Come in. How many buzzers did you ring?"

"Oh, only four or five. I told them I was a sexual goods salesman and the first few hung up on me."

"Oh, God."

"I'm joking. I only pressed one button and a kind lady told me your flat number and opened the street door. I'm on my best behaviour today because we're going to my nephew's baptism party."

"We?"

"Yes, my brother told me that I could bring somebody along and I've chosen you."

"Your brother the electrician? Didn't he mean for you to take a girl?"

"Yes and I don't know. I don't see why. Come on, it's a lovely day, not too hot, and we have to be at the restaurant by one."

"Not the church?"

"No, my brother is an atheist so he doesn't mind who turns up there."

"I haven't got a suit."

"Hmm, you can't go in that towel, although it would be fun. Do you have a shirt and tie?"

"Yes, and a jacket."

"Perfect. By the way, do you want to go? I didn't ask."

"Yes, of course."

If truth be told I didn't feel like going at all, but he was in high spirits and I didn't want to let him down. I'd never been to a wholly Spanish celebration of this kind either, so it would be a weekend of new experiences. I asked him to wait in the untidy lounge while I showered, shaved and dressed. When I emerged I found him exploring the empty bedrooms.

"You look splendid, Adam," he said, though I certainly didn't feel it. "I see that you have three extra bedrooms."

I told him about my arrangement with the landlord and that I preferred not to bother finding any flatmates. "I prefer to live alone and the rent is cheap," I said, which was true back then before the housing bubble began to inflate.

"Today I want to speak to my brother about going back to work with him. That is part of the reason why I want him to see that I have sensible friends."

"Thanks," I said, the previous day's piss up flashing before my eyes.

"If I start work and things go well, I may think about moving out of my parents' flat," he said, glancing around the small bedroom he was in.

"Right, but you'll have to see if things work out first," I said, buying myself time to think. "And you'll have to give up your benefit payments, won't you?"

"Eventually, yes, but my brother usually pays me in cash," he said, raising his eyebrows.

"You might get caught."

"This is Spain. Everybody does it." He ran his fingers over the dusty bedspread.

"Listen, you're welcome to use any of the bedrooms here. The one giving onto the street is the best spare one," I said, pointing down the gloomy passage to the room furthest from mine.

"That's very kind of you, Adam. I've never lived anywhere except my parents' flat."

"But you don't have to move out as such. Why not use the room and see how you feel about it? Stay over sometimes, bring a few things. You don't have to pay me anything until you're settled at work," I said, hoping he would read between the lines.

He nodded slowly before bringing up his dark eyes to meet mine. "I know what you're thinking, Adam. You're thinking that such a radical change of habits will not be good for my mental state; that I may not always be so... stable and that I might cause you problems."

"No, but-"

"Fear not." He held up his large hands. "Fear not because your fears are justified."

"What do you mean?"

"If I've reached the age of thirty-three without ever having lived outside the family home we both know that there's a reason for it. I think your idea is a very good one. To be able to stay here sometimes would be wonderful for me. My mother watches television all day long and that is one of the things that drives me out to the bars. But...," he paused for effect, "if I become... if my behaviour becomes peculiar, you can send me back there without further ado."

"I'm sure-"

"No, you've only known me for a short time and have not seen my little ups and downs. For now the use of the room is greatly appreciated and I may bring one or two things round this week. I'll pay you rent, of course."

"We'll talk about that later. I'll get a key made."

"Thank you. Today you'll also meet my parents. That is good."

"Will I? Is it?"

"Yes, it's their grandchild who has been baptised, after all."

"Of course."

"And it's good because I want you to meet them, and, especially, them to meet *you*. I have never had such a sensible friend before."

"Thanks," I said, beginning to tire of the adjective. I imagined, *'Here lies Adam Lowell, a sensible man'* etched on my tombstone, but then reflected that taking in Antonio as a lodger was not the act of a sensible man. Risky, rash, foolhardy, maybe compassionate, but hardly sensible.

As we drove through Murcia to the satellite town of Churra I wondered if Antonio had planned the morning's events down to the last detail. I concluded that he probably hadn't thought about the room until he had seen so many empty ones, but that the main objective of the invitation was to introduce me to his family. I had no inclination to drink much, so there was no danger of them seeing me as anything but a good influence in that respect.

He pulled into the car park of a large, no-frills restaurant and combed his hair before we made our way over to a gathering of about forty people standing and sitting under a large awning. I felt a little underdressed in my cheap jacket and decided it would look better hung over my arm. Antonio exchanged brief greetings with a few people as he sought out his brother.

"Pedro, I'd like you to meet my friend, Adam," he said to a man of forty who didn't look too comfortable in his impeccable blue suit. "Adam, this is my brother, Pedro."

Pedro looked me up and down as we shook hands and I thought I'd better say something to remove the worried expression from his face. "Hello, Pedro. Your brother and I do a lot of walking together."

"Ah, walking."

"Yes, up in the hills."

"I'm thinking about renting a room in Adam's flat, Pedro," said Antonio.

"Really?" He looked at me again.

"Yes, Adam is a good influence on me. He hardly drinks and is something of an intellectual, as well as a sportsman."

My aching head and groaning stomach didn't agree with this statement, but it seemed to produce the desired effect.

"Ah, you have made a decent friend at last. What do you do, Adam?" Pedro said, his until then impassive face brightening somewhat.

"I'm a language teacher. I believe you're an electrician?"

"Yes, and a very busy one at the moment, but," he looked around him, "one has to pay for things like this." He shrugged and neither of us knew what else to say.

"Adam, come and meet my parents," said Antonio with perfect timing.

He led me over to an elderly-looking couple, though probably not much over sixty, who were seated at a table at the edge of the patio. The stout man, much shorter than his sons, seemed even less at home in his Sunday best than Pedro, while his equally plump wife looked benevolently on at the dozen or so scampering children. To me they looked like country folk who had gone to seed in a city flat. To them I think I looked like a strange choice of companion for their son to bring to a family baptism party.

"Mother, father, this is my good friend, Adam, a language teacher."

His father pushed himself to his feet, took my hand in a firm grasp, and sat down again. His mother smiled and nodded, but neither of them looked at me for longer than they had to.

"Adam is a good friend. He keeps me out of the bars. We often go walking together," said the son, without getting much of a response. "He has also introduced me to some nice girls; educated girls," he added.

This masterstroke succeeded in removing the horrific thought that was surely passing through both their minds and the relief was palpable on both their faces. To their generation, inviting a male friend to a family celebration of this kind would have been unthinkable, I guessed, but the mention of girls changed my presence from an execrable blot to just one more of their son's foibles.

"A teacher, eh?" said the father. "I hope you can teach this son of mine a bit of common sense."

"Oh, he has plenty of that," I said, as relieved as they were by their son's clarification. "It just needs channelling in the right direction."

"I'm thinking about asking Pedro if I can go back to work for him," said Antonio.

"After last time?" said his mother, before turning to me. "He worked with Pedro for a whole year the last time until one day he decided to turn up for work dressed as a priest."

"Only the collar and shirt, mother. I wore my work trousers and boots."

"Pedro hates priests. It's a miracle that he has allowed his son to be baptised," she said. I thought she was going to cross herself but she didn't. "Anyway, he sent this one home to change and he didn't return that day."

"I thought I had discovered my calling," said Antonio.

"He had stopped taking his medication," said his father.

"He carried on acting oddly and Pedro had to let him go," said his mother.

"Since I've known him, he's been fine. I think outdoor exercise is good for him," I said, recalling our single walk in the hills, the Chinese meal, the drinking and the karate demonstrations.

At this point there was much scraping of metal chairs and people began to head into the dining room. When we had shuffled inside Antonio led me to a table at the back of the room.

"You've made a good impression, Adam, thank you. Now that's done we can start drinking some of this lovely beer and wine."

"I hardly drink, remember."

"I'll keep your glass half-full."

Our fellow guests at the round table seemed to comprise friends of Pedro and his wife, who I was yet to meet, and I was grateful that Antonio hadn't subjected me to a tableful of close relatives. A glass of beer and a bite to eat made me feel better and I looked forward to an hour or two of relaxation. Antonio filled another of my glasses with white wine and his own for the second time.

"Take it easy," I whispered. "You still have to ask your brother about going back to work for him."

"*With* him," he said, waving a forkful of prawns. "I am nobody's slave."

A single glass of wine appeared to have changed his demeanour and I resolved to monitor how much he drank. The other people at the table, mostly couples, were all engaged in conversation and I had my friend's undivided attention.

"Have you taken your medication today?"

"Yes."

"Tell me, when you drink is it best to have taken it or not to have taken it?"

He finished his second glass. "That, Adam, is a good question." He widened his eyes and smiled. "I have experimented with both methods."

"Why not experiment with not drinking?"

"It's a shame to waste such a lavish banquet," he said, spreading his arms wide over the table and raising a few eyebrows.

"Take it easy, then speak to your brother, and we can go on somewhere else afterwards," I said, watching him polish off another glass of wine. "Or do as you please."

He did as he pleased. By the time he had moved onto the red wine with the main course – a selection of meat and vegetables on communal platters – he had our table's full attention.

"My friend Adam here is a great walker," he said. "He walks and walks, but does he ever arrive?"

Assuming the question to be rhetorical, nobody replied. I cast sideways glances at him and smiled patiently, striving to give the impression that what he said should be taken with a pinch of salt.

"Do we ever arrive?" he went on, addressing a timid-looking young woman opposite him.

"I don't know," she said, glancing at her husband for support.

"Arrive where?" asked the brawny man. He was deeply tanned, from the building site rather than the beach, judging from his calloused hands, and probably not much given to philosophising.

"Where indeed?" Antonio said, before falling silent and beginning to eat with relish.

We got through to dessert without any mishaps, but when coffee and liqueurs were served a slim, bespectacled man to his left who had also drunk deeply began to needle him.

"Antonio," he said, grinning over his whisky glass, "I saw you on San Antón Street dressed in a judo suit last Thursday."

"A karate suit. Yes, on Thursdays I have my class near there."

"Is it not customary to change into street clothes after class? The children you were talking to were dressed normally."

"Ah, my little classmates, no doubt." He smiled and sipped his brandy. "Their parents make them change afterwards, but I choose to wear my suit whenever I please. I would have worn it today, but... chose not to."

"So you are in the children's class, then?" the man said, trying to get a laugh now that the end of the meal was in sight.

"Anybody can attend, but they are mostly much younger than me, yes." He looked at me and narrowed his eyes before facing his inquisitor more squarely. "So, Raúl, I take it you are still in the local police force?"

"Yes."

"Now *that* is a uniform that I would not choose to wear."

"Don't worry, they wouldn't have you," said Raúl, earning himself a chuckle or two.

"Karate, you see, is all about the harmony between the body, mind and spirit. Your job, on the other hand, is about oppression; oppression and parking tickets." This produced a good deal of laughter which did not please Raúl the cop, possibly because the local police are considered the lowliest of the three forces in Spain.

"It's time you grew up, Antonio," he said. "Playing at martial arts with kids at your age is pathetic." His partner tugged his sleeve, but Antonio's condescending smile only increased his anger. "Get a job like the rest of us."

"The matter of employment is in hand. As for the children, they are the future. I hope none of my karate colleagues are unfortunate enough to end up being policemen."

Raúl made a slight but abrupt movement towards him. On retrospect I'm sure it was just a gesture and didn't warrant Antonio's hand shooting out and grasping him around the throat. He's quite a strong-looking man, but normally so languid that I was as surprised by his swift and aggressive movement as Raúl was. Raúl went white and Antonio released him. Then Raúl went red and sprang to his feet, bumping the table as he stood and upsetting a few glasses.

"You fucking nutcase, you should be locked up! Think yourself lucky that all your family are here." He stomped away without looking back and all eyes – and I mean *all* eyes – were on my friend. He gave a little shrug, righted his spilt brandy glass and poured himself another.

"I think you might be as well to talk to your brother about work another day," I said.

"Yes, conditions are no longer ideal."

Forty minutes later we were seated at the bar in the Coyote. Antonio was drinking coffee and feeling contrite.

"Well, that wasn't a success," he said, the effects of his rapid drinking having all but disappeared after the slow drive back to Infante.

"Not really. Is that Raúl chap a good friend of your brother's?"

"An old friend rather than a good one. My brother likes policemen as little as he likes priests."

"Perhaps all is not lost, then. Tell your brother that he was offensive and that when you grabbed him you were only joking."

"Ah, Adam, sometimes I cannot control my impulses."

"You should lay off the drink for a while. It can't be good to mix medication and alcohol."

"An explosive cocktail," he said, sipping his coffee and looking glum.

"To be honest, your coming to stay at the flat worries me," I said, sensing the time was right for a few home truths.

"I see. You don't want me around."

"Not at all. I'd be delighted to see more of you, but I want it to be something constructive. Also, I don't want to upset the neighbours. The flat is cheap and, since I got rid of the other tenants, very quiet. I don't want to lose it."

He nodded, sipped, and nodded again. "From today, from now, I will have a break from alcohol. Look, there is your friend Dominic."

Dominic was walking around the bar stealing surreptitious glances in our direction. Maybe because we were smartly dressed and looking solemn he risked taking a seat by my side. He looked as hungover as I had felt six hours earlier and didn't speak until he had taken his first tentative sip of beer.

"Have you two been to a funeral?"

"No, a baptism. Antonio's nephew," I said. "Have you two met before?" I asked, looking from one to the other guilelessly.

Dominic reached across the bar in front of me and Antonio took his hand.

"Pleased to meet you," he said, managing his first smile since we had left the lunch party.

"Likewise," said Dominic, and we all lapsed into silence.

Having drunk two or three glasses of wine at lunch I was feeling fairly cheerful and decided that it was up to me to make the most of this overdue meeting of my two friends.

"Dominic works at the electrical supplies shop down the street," was the only common ground I could come up with at such short notice.

"Ah, I'm an electrician, although not fully qualified. I'll be returning to work soon, now that I have given up alcohol."

Dominic nodded and looked at Antonio more closely. "I too am going to begin to drink less. At my age one has to begin to lead a more sober life," he said before taking a sip of beer.

Had Antonio's statement made Dominic believe that his odd behaviour was solely due to drink? I certainly wasn't going to disabuse him of that idea. I eased my stool back a few inches to allow the two repentant soaks to speak more freely. Dominic spoke about his drumming and Antonio mentioned his karate. They compared ages and agreed that physical activity became increasingly important as one got older. Dominic said he wished to supplement his vigorous drumming sessions with some other form of exercise. Antonio said that you couldn't beat walking in the mountains and would he join us on our next excursion the following Saturday? Dominic said he certainly would if it didn't clash with his drumming class with the great Pedrín.

"Do you know Pedrín, the drummer of the Marañones?" he asked him.

"I know of him, yes," said Antonio.

Dominic whipped out his phone and pressed a rapid dial button. "Pedrín, hello, it's Dominic. Could we have a class this evening?

Yes? Great. Shall we meet in La Bomba at seven? Good, see you then."

"Have you had many classes?" Antonio asked.

"Er, not as many as I should. I'll take classes three times a week from now on. I'll save money for them by drinking less of this." He held up his bottle. "Would you both like to come to see my class?"

I waited for Antonio to speak.

"Not today, Dominic. I have to sort out some things at home, but another day I'd be delighted to come."

"At least come over to La Bomba to meet him."

Antonio's face clouded and I apprised Dominic of his poor reception there on his only visit.

"What? What nonsense! Troco cannot treat my friends like that. We will go there now and if his attitude is bad I will never set foot in that hole again." He finished his beer and his foot began to tap rapidly on the footrest.

I looked at Antonio and was relieved to see a smile appear on his face.

"Now that I do not drink or arrange my things on the bar I should be able to enter any establishment, shouldn't I?"

Dominic marched us across the street and square and ushered us in through the door. Troco was perfectly amenable to Antonio's presence, only regretting that he did not possess a coffee machine. He ordered a coke and Dominic and I followed suit.

"Pichas, what is this?" Troco said with a cackle. "Smart clothes, no drinking. Have you found religion, or what?"

"One must begin to care for one's body at our age, Troco," said Dominic solemnly. "You ought to smoke less of that stuff, too."

"Picha, smoking weed never did anyone any harm," he said, holding up the joint he had just rolled. "Have you ever see people fighting after smoking? No. Have you ever see people ranting and raving and doing crazy things after smoking? Not often. Smoking is the future," he said, and then after a thoughtful pause, "Of course there's no need to stop drinking altogether. A few beers is no bad thing."

"Here, you mean?" said Dominic.

"Of course, picha."

We all had a good laugh about this. When Pedrín arrived and refused a coke point blank we all laughed some more. After the inauspicious events at the baptism party everything had turned out well. We were all friends. We were all going to lead healthier, more constructive lives. Today was a great turning point, Dominic told us, and Antonio agreed. Pedrín observed all this camaraderie impassively as he sipped his beer and smoked. Something in his expression told me that he thought our optimism might be based on shaky foundations.

8

When I opened Jed's bar the following Thursday evening I hadn't heard from my two new friends all week, and when I closed it neither of them had put in an appearance. I was reflecting on these long silences as I crossed the bridge over the river to my flat and only then did it occur to me that I hadn't phoned or texted them either.

What did that say about my attitude towards them? Why did I always expect them to contact me? In the case of Dominic I considered my wait-and-see approach justified due to his capricious habits, but Antonio might be waiting for a word of encouragement regarding his wish to make use of my flat.

I realised that I was starting to see myself as some sort of mentor, a steadying influence who was approachable but who would not make the first move. Was this not presumptuous of me? Even rather arrogant? I reflected that all friendships were a question of give and take and that each party normally did more of one thing than the other. What, after all, did I stand to gain from associating with either of those mercurial characters?

Well, for one thing a chance to integrate more into Murcian life. For the latter half of my three years in Valencia I'd had a Spanish girlfriend and had met most of her friends and some of her family. She was a sensible girl and most of the people she knew were rather dull, but at least through her I met local people and practiced – dare I say perfected? – my Spanish. When we split up I decided that a change of airs was desirable, so, making use of a few language school contacts, I moved south to Murcia and set up on my own.

Although I got on well enough with some of my adult students, I had so far felt no desire to take my association with any of them beyond the classroom walls. As a consequence, my social life had revolved around expat teaching circles and as far as integration was concerned I felt I was going backwards rather than forwards.

Then Dominic and Antonio had appeared on the scene – or I had appeared on their scene – and I had to admit that life had become more interesting. The six hours I had just spent in Jed's bar had been dull and most of the conversations predictable. I had no intention of returning there over the weekend unless Jed called me to help him out, and I was counting on either or both of my new friends to entertain me. That was the long and short of it and I decided that I'd better start being more grateful for the friendship they had offered me so willingly.

The next day I finished my last class of the week at twelve o'clock and sent Antonio a text message as I was walking along Gran Vía towards the bridge. When I turned onto my street I saw him approaching from the other direction. He was carrying a travel bag and I doubted that the quarter hour that had elapsed would have given him time to pack it.

"So you're moving in?" I said, smiling broadly.

"I've just thrown a few things into this bag in case I stay over one night."

"Let's leave it upstairs and go and get a key cut."

We entered the flat and I made for the front bedroom.

"It's all yours. There are sheets and blankets in that cupboard and I'll put that bedspread in the washing machine."

"Thank you, but I've brought some sheets," he said, opening the bag. As well as the light-green sheets and pillow slips he extracted two towels, a good deal of clothing, two pairs of shoes, a small radio, a toiletry bag and a couple of books. Only the absence of the karate suit told me that he intended to return to the family flat at some point.

"Shall we go and get that key cut?"

"First I will mop the floor, if I may."

"Yes, and we'd better clean all the drawers. What are you reading?"

"Oh, science fiction. I prefer other worlds to this one." He smiled and seemed very serene.

"Are you still off the drink?"

"Yes, since Sunday I've tried the full medication and no alcohol method. I've been drowsy all week. From today I will try another way; no medication and just a little alcohol."

"Is that wise?"

"We will see, but I'm sick of feeling drugged all the time. The doctors only wish to keep me half-asleep, but I want to live."

In half an hour we cleaned the room and Antonio made his bed. He lay down on it and smiled up at me. "This is the first time I've stretched out on a bed other than my own for several years. Most men do military services, but I was exempted."

"Consider the room yours," I said, realising that he had made very few references to girls since I had met him. I would have to quiz him about his love life when the time was right.

We got a key cut and bought a bulb for the bedside lamp at the hardware store on Cartagena Street. I suggested we eat a light lunch in the flat, before going for a walk along the river, my normal Friday routine from September onwards.

"Hmm, it will be a little hot for walking until the evening. I'd like to buy you lunch at the Chinese restaurant and perhaps we could go for a walk later."

My liking for May and June prevailed over my lack of enthusiasm for Chinese cuisine and I agreed. "But it's my turn to pay this time."

"Absolutely not. We must celebrate your kindness in allowing me to make occasional use of your flat and I insist on paying," he said with finality.

It was a relief to get out of the glare of the sun and May and June seemed genuinely pleased to see us. The few other customers looked like they would be returning to work soon and I looked forward to chatting to the girls later. Antonio ordered his usual zhajiangmian for starter and I went for spring rolls. I toyed with my beer, but he soon finished his and ordered a bottle of red wine with the main course. May's eyes danced as he bantered with her and when she returned to the kitchen I asked him if he liked her.

"Oh yes, and June too, but especially May."

"Have you ever thought about asking her out?"

"No, I would never ask her out. The cultural divide is too great. I did ask her to marry me once, but she didn't take my proposal seriously." He chuckled at the thought.

"Are there any other girls... on the horizon? Anyone you like?"

"Ah, you've decided to quiz me about my feelings for the fair sex, I see," he said, fork suspended in mid-air.

"I was just wondering."

"I am not gay, if that's what you're thinking."

"No, I didn't think so," I said, managing to avoid following up with, 'and I wouldn't mind if you were'.

"My success with the ladies has been limited, Adam, due, I suppose, to my peculiar ways."

"Don't some women like men who are... out of the ordinary?"

"Some do, at first. Oh, I've had my successes from a sexual point of view, but when I've wished for more I always seem to frighten them away. Only two or three months ago I invited a girl to lunch who appealed to me a lot. She arrived with a male friend, which surprised me, but I took them to a good restaurant all the same. As the meal progressed I saw them exchanging looks each time I made one of my little jokes and when I'd paid the bill they thanked me and left. When I drove away I saw them kissing in the street."

"That's bad."

"I was very disappointed; in her and in myself for being so naïve." He took a long drink of wine and looked down at his plate.

"How did the karate go yesterday?" I asked, preferring not to broach the subject of my own lack of success with the fair sex since my arrival in Murcia.

"Oh, fine. There with the young people I'm in my element. They sometimes laugh at me, but they're also fond of me. Children do not lie and deceive as adults do."

"You should work with them. Become a teacher or something."

"I would like that very much, but, alas, with my history of mental health problems it would be impossible."

"I guess so."

"I'd also have to study a lot. Ha!" he cried, startling me and the other diners. "Let us toast to our friendship and look towards the future." We clinked our glasses and emptied them. "I perceive that you haven't met any interesting girls lately."

"Not really, no."

"That's strange, because you're quite handsome and very steady and sensible. Most girls like men like you."

"Yes, but the problem is that the ones who like me are a bit too sensible themselves. Sensible and boring."

"And you will marry one someday, I am sure. But," he raised his voice again before letting it fall to a murmur, "in the meantime we will drink and forget our disappointments."

I hadn't been planning to drink much at all that weekend, let alone at Friday lunch, but I didn't want to appear ungrateful for the invite and the chance to chat with the girls. Sure enough, when she had served us our coffee and brandy, May took up her position behind the spare chair.

"Sit down and rest your legs, May. There are no other customers left," said Antonio.

After popping her head through the kitchen doors and taking a bottle of water from the display fridge she sat down and pushed her chair a little way from the table. She seemed smaller and more delicate seated and I thought it a pity that she had to work seven days a week in the restaurant.

"Do you ever take a break, May, and go on holiday?" I asked.

"Yes, two summers ago my mother and I went back to China for a month."

"To see your family?"

"Of course. To my village in Guangxi, not far from the coast."

"Do you not miss it?"

"Not really. It was good to visit, but the standard of life is poor there. Buying a new fridge is a big event for most people. Here we are much better off."

"Adam is now thinking that you work too much, but doesn't feel able to approach the subject directly," said my friend. "He is more diplomatic than me."

"Yes, and he drinks less, although not much. We Chinese are very industrious. I prefer to be busy here than poor there."

"Adam has kindly allowed me to use a room in his flat in order to spend some time away from my parents, and their television."

Rather than applauding his bid for independence, her brow furrowed and she glanced at me briefly. "I'm not sure if that's a good idea, Antonio."

"Why not?" I said, surprised at her reaction. "He won't have to spend so much time in the bars if he has a place of his own. I'm out working most of the day, so he'll be able to do his own thing."

"Like what?"

"Well, read and… practise his karate moves and… things like that."

"But now you are both here, already drinking. Will you return to the flat now?"

"Yes, unless we go for a walk along the river."

"Ha, or to the pubs. You will not be good for each other," she said with a quick shake of the head and a quizzical glance in my direction.

I interpreted this look as meaning that Antonio would not be good for me. I can't be sure of this, but whether she meant it or not it got me thinking. Instead of being half way down the riverside path towards Alcantarilla I was half way to getting drunk again. Would I end up spending even more of my spare time in bars than I did already?

As well as serving me lunch she had also given me food for thought and I decided to store away that Chinese wisdom for future use. There was little I could do with it that afternoon, however, as Antonio had paid the bill and convinced me that the best place to allow our lunch to settle would be at the bar in the Coyote.

"May has got a point," I said once we were there. I had ordered another coffee and I wanted to get a few things straight.

"May is wise beyond her years," he said, swirling his brandy and looking into it.

"I mean, I don't really want to spend more time in bars than I already do."

"You are free to go, Adam. I won't bother you when I come in."

"No, well, this is a one-off, but she's just made me think," I said, finishing my coffee and ordering a beer. "What do you think of Dominic?" I asked.

"Yes, let's change the subject. Dominic? Oh, I don't know. He's a kind person, I believe, but I think he lacks... depth."

"Depth?"

"Yes, I don't know him well, but I think he goes from one enthusiasm to another and he won't grow old gracefully."

"Hmm, I think you may be right, but, well..."

"You didn't expect to hear that from me, of all people."

"It's not that, but-"

"Adam, please," he snapped. "Be honest. If we cannot be honest then what is the use of our friendship?"

"All right, I will. I'm not at all surprised that you've come to that conclusion because I think the same. What surprises me is that you say it so complacently as if you, or I, were any different."

"But we are different; from Dominic and from each other. You have your career and, as I said, I think one day you'll meet a nice, pretty girl and settle down. You'll drink less as you get older and will do the usual things that healthy, cultured people do. You'll have children, take trips, enjoy the countryside, read good books; in short, you'll have a happy and rewarding life. You'll look back on the time you spent in Murcia with fondness, and on me too, I hope."

"Will I leave Murcia?"

"Adam, I am not a mind reader."

"And what about you?"

"Ah, now that is a more difficult question. You're right to think that if I continue on my current path that my future and Dominic's will not differ greatly. But, I have the hope that one day I'll get this straight." He tapped his forehead. "I'll get this straight and I may one day achieve something."

"I'll help you as much as I can," I said, feeling quite moved.

"I know and I thank you. Now you can order me a beer. I want no more strong drink today."

"How do you feel without the medication?"

"Different. Fine, but different. Next week I'll dispense with both medication and alcohol."

"What will you do… with your time."

"On Monday I'll go to the library."

After a pensive half hour over our beers we walked over to La Bomba and our sombre mood belied the fact that we had drunk quite a bit that afternoon. Troco didn't seem to notice and nor did Dominic when he walked in ten minutes later to have, he said, a quick one after work.

"After this I'm going home," he said when he'd ordered a beer. "Tomorrow at four I have a drum class with Pedrín. Would you like to come?"

We both said we would and I checked that I still had the map he had drawn for me in my wallet. "Do you fancy coming for a walk tomorrow morning, Dominic? We'll set off at about eight," I said. I hadn't mentioned this to Antonio, but I thought it a good way of letting him know that I wasn't about to change my weekend habits.

"At eight o'clock? I don't think so, Adam. Not that I won't be able to, because, as I said, I am going home now, but I must be fresh for my class tomorrow."

"How are you getting on with Don Quixote?"

"Not bad. I've finished chapter five. The peasant has just taken him home in a battered state and they've put him to bed. I read slowly, but I'm enjoying it."

"Yes, it's best not to rush it," I said, recalling that there were at least fifty chapters in the first part and even more in the second. It might take him two or three years to finish it, but at least he was reading a great book.

While Troco was blowing the smoke from his joint through the hatch into the square I told Dominic that we were going to have couple of quiet beers over at Jed's bar.

"All right, I'll come too, but we must leave separately," he whispered.

"Why?"

"Troco will be offended. It's Friday, so he'll know we are going elsewhere."

"It's a free country, isn't it?" I murmured, watching Troco's back.

Antonio observed this cowardly exchange with a smile on his face that told me something was brewing in that head of his. I could see that he was waiting for Troco to return from the hatch.

"Come on, boys," he said when the owner had settled down on a stool opposite us to enjoy the effects of the joint. "They are expecting us at Jed's bar. We don't want the party to start without us and there might not be enough of those foreign girls to go round."

I looked at my watch and finished my beer while Dominic sat like a schoolboy waiting for a rap on the knuckles. Then he remembered his alibi.

"Not me. As I said," he enunciated carefully, "I am just having this one and going home."

I persuaded Antonio that it was neither practical nor necessary to drive into the tascas and a quarter of an hour later we were seated at the table nearest to the bar. Dominic arrived shortly after looking like he'd just escaped from a maximum security prison.

"Did he suspect?" Antonio asked him.

"Suspect? I told him I was going home and he wished me a happy evening at Jed's bar," he said, shaking his head and chuckling. "But you're right, Antonio. It's not our fault that his bar isn't going well and that there are never any pretty girls there, apart from his girlfriend. Still, Antonio, you could have been more subtle about it."

"I owed him one."

"Hi, you guys," said Jed, appearing at our side. He sometimes greeted newcomers in English to prove that it was an authentic American bar. 'It seems exotic to these Murcians,' he once told me.

"Jed, you've met Dominic. This is Antonio, another good friend of mine."

"Hi, Antonio, nice to meet you," he said, now in his American Spanish. "How did you meet this crazy English guy?"

"It is I who am crazy, not Adam," he said.

"Nor me," said Dominic.

Antonio had made this statement in such a deadpan manner that Jed was nonplussed. At that moment my erstwhile drinking pals, Richard, Geoff and Simon, came in and Jed headed back behind the bar. I nodded to them as they passed and listened to their chatter as they prepared for another exciting night out. I suppose I should have introduced them to my companions, but as none of them came over to the table I didn't bother. Theirs seemed like another world now, one I could find in any European city, and I was sure they wouldn't have much in common with my two Infante friends.

I'll admit that I was relieved that both Dominic and Antonio were in an especially rational frame of mind, though I knew that could change at any moment. It was a quiet night in the end and my two pals continued to chat with great self-possession until we said our goodbyes at midnight. Perhaps they were sizing each other up, or perhaps they just didn't feel at home in the half-student, half-professional atmosphere of the tascas. For me Jed's bar had become a place where I preferred to earn money rather than spend it.

9

At four o'clock on the following afternoon I walked into a setting that was completely unfamiliar to me. The hustle and bustle of musicians in and around the warren of soundproof rehearsal rooms in the old warehouse on the Santomera road was a far cry from a Friday night in the tascas. After an unpromising start to the day, I was glad we had come.

I had gone walking alone that morning, for an hour down the river after getting up at ten, and when I returned Antonio was emerging from the bathroom, dripping water along the passage.

"Did you sleep well?" I asked.

"Quite well, yes. The bed seemed very big, but comfortable." He sat on it in his towel, looking a little out of sorts.

"Did the light not bother you? I know the curtains aren't very thick and the room gets the sun in the mornings."

"Yes, I may buy an eye mask. Tell me, who was the last person to live in this room?"

"The last person to sleep here was a friend from England who came for the weekend."

"Yes, but who was the last person to *live* here?"

"Er, a chap called Alejandro. He worked as a cook."

"The room has a strange atmosphere. Was he happy here?"

"I don't really know. I'll make some coffee while you get dressed," I said, leaving the room.

Alejandro had been in the flat when I arrived there and our paths rarely crossed, which was fine by me. He was pleasant enough when we did coincide and when he emerged from his room one morning with another man it didn't bother me. Each to their own, I thought, but when the downstairs neighbour told me there had been a lot of shouting and scraping of furniture one evening I became a little concerned. Then one Sunday after returning from a weekend away I found an envelope addressed to me had been pushed under the door.

It was from the downstairs neighbour, an elderly lady, asking me to call. I went down and she told me about the dramatic events of the previous night. There had been more shouting and scuffling, which had continued into the lift, and when she went to inspect it she found the walls smeared with blood. She had rung the landlord, who she knew well, and he had ejected Alejandro that same day. I was glad I had chosen that weekend to go away.

"The atmosphere of the room is a little disturbing," Antonio said as he joined me in the kitchen, looking a bit disturbed himself.

I told him about Alejandro.

"Ah, I suspected something of the kind."

"There are two more rooms," I said. "One next to mine and one between the toilet and the bathroom."

"Who lived in them last?"

"In the one next to mine there was a young man called Amadeo when I arrived."

"A strange name for a young man."

"And a strange young man. He was extremely polite and said he was a student at the university, but he spent up to sixteen hours at a time in his room, without making a sound."

"Sixteen hours?"

"Yes, at least. He would be in there when I arrived home at, say, nine o'clock and one Saturday he didn't emerge until two, unless he got up while I was asleep. It was disturbing to have him there right next to me all the time, never making a sound."

"What happened to him?"

"He moved back to his village shortly after Alejandro left, perhaps because of all the trouble. After those two I decided against having any more flatmates, until now, that is."

"And the other room?"

"It hasn't been used since I've been here."

Antonio left the kitchen and returned a moment later. "I think I'll use that room, if you don't mind."

"That's fine by me, but it's very small and dark."

"Just like my room at home. I'll have lunch with my parents and return at half past three with some smaller bedsheets." He sipped his coffee and stared at the fridge.

"Are you feeling all right?"

"I'll be fine."

When he picked me up later he was more cheerful and seemed just as interested as I was in the comings and goings of the musicians as they prepared for their rehearsals. They were mostly young, hairy types, but there were some older men too and a couple of women, all looking purposeful as they carried their instrument cases to their respective rooms. We waited in the office cum bar and I soon saw Dominic waving his drumsticks over the heads of those around us.

"Come on, Pedrín's waiting. I've already bought the litres."

He led us along a corridor where the muffled sound of groups already in action could be heard and into a small, windowless room almost completely occupied by two drum kits. Pedrín lifted a drumstick in acknowledgement of our arrival while Dominic ushered us to the two plastic chairs and handed me a litre bottle of beer. He sat down on his drum stool, checked the position of his drums and cymbals, and turned to Pedrín with a look of intense, almost comic, concentration on his face.

"I'm ready, maestro," he said, without so much as tapping a cymbal.

By the end of the class proper, which lasted about forty-five minutes, I knew a little more about drumming than before I entered the room, but I won't try to describe all the exercises that Pedrín put Dominic through. It wasn't at all as I'd imagined it. I'd expected Pedrín to hammer away on the drums and for Dominic to copy him, but it wasn't like that at all.

Much of the time was spent beating a simple rhythm on a single drum. It looked easy, but Pedrín was continually correcting his pupil. Learning to play the drums clearly required a lot of patience and concentration and I began to see why Dominic often left long gaps between classes. For a man of his temperament it must have been frustrating, but he tried his best and was visibly drained by the end of it.

Pedrín had been patience personified and, being a teacher myself, I knew that it would have been much easier to humour Dominic by letting him bang away to his heart's content, just like I let my intermediate students gabble on when I was too tired to correct them.

"That's enough for today," Pedrín said when he saw that Dominic could take no more. "You two have a go if you like, but please take care of my drums."

He left the room and Dominic took a long swig of beer, before moving over to Pedrín's well-worn kit and immediately striking up the same beat that I'd heard on the previous Saturday. His face beamed with relief and I couldn't help thinking that anything new that his motor neurons had learnt would soon be lost as he forced them back into the same old groove.

"Have a go, Antonio," he said. "See if you can do this."

Antonio sat down behind Dominic's drum kit and after a few tentative taps began to replicate his beat.

"That's good," Dominic shouted. "You must have had lessons."

"A few when I was younger, but this is all I can play."

Rather than being disturbed by this piece of news, Dominic bashed on happily for a while, before standing and handing me the sticks. "Take good care of the maestro's kit," he said.

"I don't think I'll break it," I replied, before tapping all of the drums to see how they sounded. I watched Antonio and tried to copy him, but I couldn't coordinate my right foot with my hands and soon gave it up.

Antonio stopped shortly afterwards and the silence was a great relief.

"It's not as easy as it looks, eh?" said Dominic after finishing one of the litre bottles. "I'm sure Pedrín would be happy to give you classes."

"Not for me, but he's a good teacher. You should stick at it," I said.

"Yes, I should. Shall we go to La Bomba now or to Luis's house?"

"To La Bomba, please," said Pedrín, who had opened the door as soon as we had stopped.

"You could teach Lucky a few tricks," I said.

"I could, and I have done in the past, but I cannot support the presence of Alberto."

"Isn't he a real pro?" I asked.

"In his own head, yes, but his arrogance is far from justified. Now, Antonio, do you drive more slowly than Dominic?"

"I drive slowly," he said.

"Then I will come with you."

Dominic went home for a shower after his exertions and the three of us drove back into Murcia. La Bomba was almost empty when we arrived and I bought a round of beer. Pedrín and I had chatted on the way there, but Antonio hadn't said a word. Not wishing to ask him how he was feeling again, I was glad when Pedrín addressed him.

"So, Antonio, you have played the drums before?"

"A few lessons when I was a teenager, nothing more."

"It's not for everyone, and you need somewhere for the drums. I'm lucky to have my little room. I pay no rent because I teach a few youngsters there," he said, glancing at me. "What do you do with yourself nowadays?" he asked him.

"I've taken up karate, but I do nothing else to speak of."

"No work?"

"Not at the moment."

I wondered where this was leading and decided to remain silent.

"We all need something to keep us busy," Pedrín went on. "I'm lucky because I love drumming. I have little work at present, but I cycle out there every day to practise and to give advice to other people. I only come to the bar if I feel that I've done something worthwhile."

Antonio nodded, but made no reply. Pedrín said no more and the three of us remained silent for a while, sipping our beer.

"Thank you for that, Pedrín," Antonio said after a few minutes. "You've given me advice without following it up with a lecture. Yes, I need to find something to do. The karate is a mere amusement and will lead nowhere. Now I have a room in Adam's flat. When he goes off to work on Monday I'll have nothing to do. There will be no television to annoy me like in my family home, but I'll still have nothing to do. So what will I do? I'll go to the Chinese restaurant and then to the bars. When my money runs short I'll just go to the bars. That is no life."

At that moment Dominic entered and charged towards us with a smile on his face. I put my finger to my lips and he veered off to talk to Troco.

"I was so looking forward to getting my own space, thanks to Adam's kindness," Antonio said to Pedrín. "But when I woke up this morning I realised that it changes nothing. That's why I've been so quiet today, Adam. My concern about the room was just nonsense, although I did feel some bad vibrations in there. I *must* find something to do."

"What about working for... working with your brother?" I asked.

"Oh, it would be better than idleness, but the truth is that we don't get on and I don't find the work interesting. I pin all my hopes on feeling well enough to go back to work with him when that is not the solution."

"Find something you like doing, and the rest will take care of itself," said Pedrín. "I have suffered from depression in the past. When my group were successful there was a lot of drinking and taking drugs. I came down from that high and everything seemed hopeless. Then, little by little, I went back to my drums, on my own, just to practise. For me it's drumming, for you it will be something else. Forget your brother. If you're receiving money to live already it need not be paid work, but find something to do."

Antonio held up four fingers to Troco and lit a cigarette. Dominic soon joined us and Pedrín began to tease him about his drumming skills. For a drummer timing is of the essence, but it seemed to me that Pedrín was a master of it away from the drum kit too.

Antonio and I left La Bomba at about half past nine and decided to grab a bite to eat in the Mesón de Juan before returning to the flat. After chatting away with us all evening my friend became pensive as we walked towards the bar and I decided to take a leaf out of Pedrín's book and not interrupt his thoughts.

Despite being a Saturday, Juan's bar wasn't busy, so we sat up at the bar and ordered beer and some tapas.

"I shall ask Juan for advice when he's free," Antonio said.

"Do you know him well?"

"Of course, his bar has been here for as long as I can remember. He's seen me in good times and bad and is a sympathetic man."

"He's been nice to me too," I said, remembering the welcome he gave me when I first came to live in the area. "He always makes a sandwich for people who come in saying they are hungry. Never money, but always something to eat."

"I know."

When the time came to order coffee there were only a handful of people left in the bar. Juan made himself one too and stood opposite us.

"Ah, I'm looking forward to my day off tomorrow," he said as he stirred in the sugar. His wife Elena had already left and his brother-in-law Paco was busy cleaning up the kitchen.

"Juan, I need something to do," said Antonio.

"You can sweep the floor if you like."

"No, I mean something to do with my life... although I would be happy to sweep the floor too."

"The cleaner will do that tomorrow morning. Are you bored of martial arts already?"

"Oh, that's just a hobby. I need something to do with my life."

"Has your brother no work for you?"

"That is no longer the solution. I need something new. Something to occupy my mind and my body."

"Do you have a notebook?" Juan asked him.

"No, but-"

"I have a spare one," I said. "Antonio now stays at my flat some of the time," I told him.

"That in itself is a change. A good change, so long as you don't spend too much time in the bars," he said, his blue eyes serious. "So, take a notebook and think of everybody you know, and I mean everybody. Friends, friends of friends, family, extended family, write them all down. Adam, you could think about the people that you know too. When you cannot think of anybody else, look at the list and transfer the names of those people who lead active, happy lives to separate pages. Think some more about these people. Think about what they do and if you could not do something similar. Consider if they might be able to help you begin to do it." He looked at us as we both sat thinking. "But take your time over it, several days. The idea is to do some lateral thinking and this requires patience."

"Have you ever used this method?" I asked him.

"Yes, when I was young I was training to be a car mechanic and I didn't like it. I didn't like the oil and the dirt and spending all day with only my boss to talk to. I filled a little notebook with names and my thoughts kept returning to my Uncle Samuel who had a little bar in Mula. He wasn't well off, but always seemed happy. I went to see him one Saturday and he agreed to take me on as a kind of apprentice. My father was furious with Samuel, his brother, and told him that learning a skilled trade was better than rotting away in a bar.

"Ha, Uncle Samuel told my father that he loved his bar and his customers and that happiness was more important to him than earning a lot of money. I should try it for a year, he told him, and by then I would know if it was for me. Well, after two years with Uncle Samuel I came back to Murcia to get experience in the good restaurants and after saving for a few years I bought this bar. I've been here for almost twenty years now and I still enjoy opening each morning."

"What happened to your Uncle Samuel?" Antonio asked him.

"Oh, he's almost eighty now. His son runs the bar, but he still spends a lot of time there helping out. My father worked as a builder, made a lot of money, and died at sixty-six."

"So there's a moral to the story," I said.

"Well, that's just the way things turned out. I'm going to have a small whisky now to celebrate the end of the week. Will you join me?"

As we sipped the whisky I saw that Antonio had already begun to make a mental list and when we returned to the flat he said goodnight and took a notebook and pen to his new room. It was a nice idea, I thought, and I hoped he would find an Uncle Samuel among his relations.

10

During the next three days Antonio rarely left the flat, and when he did his notebook went with him. He didn't share the results of his labours with me, so I didn't ask. In the meantime I thought about all the people I knew, but as most of them were in England and all my Spanish-based acquaintances apart from Jed were involved in language teaching I could offer no suggestions. If Antonio thought bar work was for him I was sure that he would come up with that idea himself, but I rather hoped he wouldn't.

When I got home from my classes on Wednesday evening Antonio was sitting at the ugly dining room table peering at his already ragged notebook. As I made my way along the L-shaped passage to my room he called me back. His hands were crossed on the table and he smiled up at me.

"I think I've got it," he said.

"Go on."

"After making notes on everybody I know and thinking mainly about people who are living in different parts of Spain, I think I've found a possible solution closer to home."

"What is it? Who is it?"

"A friend of my father's."

"What does he do?"

"He's a builder."

"So you want to get into the building trade?"

"Yes and no. Not only that. My idea involves you too."

"I'm intrigued."

"My father's friend is called Mario. He's a very friendly man and he lives in a house that he built himself just off the road to Alcantarilla. He doesn't build flats; he builds houses or restores them. He likes working with stone. He's quite old now, almost sixty I think, and his two sons work with him."

"So where do you fit in? And where do I fit in?"

"A couple of months ago he was at my parents' flat drinking coffee. I remember now that he was lamenting the fact that none of his children had learnt English properly, neither his sons nor his two daughters. He said that he would love to be able to get in touch with foreign buyers and build or restore houses for them. There was a big market there, he said, and he was unable to exploit it."

"He could get some sort of agent."

"He doesn't like estate agents. He likes to keep things within the family."

"But you're not family."

"But he likes me, and my father and he were once very close."

"So what's your idea? What are you going to propose to him?" I asked, worried that whatever it was would eat into my spare time.

"First we must speak to him. We can call at his house on Saturday. You'll like him and he'll like you. His wife and children are also very nice. I'll tell him that you're English and that I also speak English quite well and I'll propose that we find him some foreign buyers."

"Do you speak English quite well? I've never asked."

"No, I don't, but I studied it at school. By the weekend, with a little help from you, I'll speak well enough to convince him that I can. After that I'll continue to study and by the time we meet some prospective buyers I'll be able to get by."

My heart sank. There is nothing worse than leaving work after teaching all day only to have to humour somebody who is trying to learn the language. It had happened to me in Valencia and I'd learnt to steer clear of people like that. Still, this was Antonio, and he was on a mission.

"Although this is only part of it," he said. "I'd also like to learn some building skills and Mario is a very nice person to be around. I think he'd let me help them out, and when possible buyers arrive I'd be there to speak to them. What do you think, Adam?"

"Well, the idea's a good one if you can attract potential buyers, but it's not so easy to learn English. I don't have much time to teach you this week."

"Don't worry about that. I have an idea for Saturday which will only take half an hour to prepare. After that, if you lend me a suitable book, I'll study alone and pay you for a few classes."

"Don't be silly, I wouldn't charge you."

"I insist. In any case, you also have a lot to gain from this project. I shan't charge Mario for helping him with the building work, but when we sell a house or get him a substantial piece of work we'll have agreed a commission with him."

This minor point perked me up somewhat. I'd known for a long time that a bilingual person could make money in the housing racket, but I hadn't a clue how to go about it. Nor did I have a car, thinking one an unnecessary expense in the city, but Antonio could supply the wheels.

"I'm beginning to like the idea," I said.

"When you meet Mario you'll like it even more." He closed the notebook and clapped his hands. "Now I am very happy," he said in English. It was a start.

When we turned off the main road and drove up the short lane to Mario's large, stone-clad house on Saturday afternoon he was already expecting us. Antonio had called him, but had not told him the reason for his visit. When we left the car and walked toward the porch a stout, smiling man was waiting at the top of the steps. As we approached him we performed the following well-rehearsed conversation in English.

"This is a nice big house," said Antonio, walking slowly and talking loudly.

"Yes, the stonework is very impressive. Did Mario do all this himself?"

"Yes, with the help of his wife María and his children, who were quite young at the time."

"It must have taken him a long time."

"About three years, I think, mainly at the weekends," he said as we reached the bottom step. "Ah, Mario, how are you?" he said in Spanish.

"Fine," he said, his fine brown eyes lit up with merriment. "What's wrong with your mouths?"

"Oh, this is my good friend, Adam. He's English, so we sometimes speak it together."

"Come in. The coffee is almost ready."

He led us to a small, round table in a corner of the huge dining room before introducing us to his wife María, a good-looking woman a few years his junior. Mario himself was short, fat, almost bald and, it has to be said, rather ugly, but his eyes were filled with benevolence. He'd made a good match and you could tell they were a happy couple. María brought in a tray of coffee and cakes and said she would return soon.

"So, to what do I owe this unexpected pleasure, Antonio? Oh, does your friend understand Spanish?"

I assured him that I did and told him that we spoke it at least half the time.

"I have a favour to ask of you, Mario," said Antonio.

"Tell me," he said without hesitation.

"I want to come to work for you, for nothing."

"*That's* a favour?"

"Yes, because I want to learn about building work, but that's not all. I remember you mentioning to my father that you'd like to be able to attract foreign customers. I think that Adam and I would be able to locate some."

Mario looked at each of us in turn, sipped his coffee, and cleared his throat. "Antonio, you look very well, but how are you feeling in yourself right now?"

"Better than I've felt for a long time, Mario, but I've decided not to go back to work with my brother Pedro. I need a new challenge and I'm keen to work with you, and with my friend Adam. I need to be around people who give me a positive feeling."

I gathered from this exchange that Mario was fully aware of Antonio's mental health issues, as we English like to call them. Our host thought for a while before clearing his throat.

"It's true that I've often regretted not being able to speak to foreigners who are interested in buying houses here. All foreigners except Germans, that is, because, as Antonio knows, I spent many years working in Germany and I get by in that language," he said to me, before looking at my friend. "However, my main concern if we went ahead with this idea would be your welfare, Antonio. I'm not a greedy man and my sons and I always have enough work, so I'll only do this if it's good for you. If I see it isn't, I will not pursue it. Adam, what do you think?"

I told him about my blossoming friendship with Antonio and that I had given him the use of a room in my flat. I told him quite frankly that I was aware of his problems, but that I thought the key was for him to have some kind of goal. I said that I thought his proposal was a good one and that I would back him up insofar as I was able. I didn't mention anything about drinking sessions, spontaneous karate demonstrations, throat grabbing, or any other odd behaviour.

"I see you're on his side and I admire your loyalty," said Mario, his eyes glittering in his deeply-tanned face. "It so happens that we're now carrying out a project where my lack of English is most annoying. We're restoring a house in the village of Villanueva del Río Segura, about thirty kilometres from Murcia. I bought the house, very cheaply, and wish to sell it when it's finished. There are a few foreign people living in the village already – English, I think – and I've seen others walking around with people who look like estate agents." He said the last two words with distaste. "If I could only speak to the foreigners who live there, perhaps I could interest their friends in the house."

"And the other houses that are for sale," I said. "If you find some foreign people who are interested you could find out who owns the houses and bypass the estate agents." I looked from Mario to Antonio, hoping I had said the right thing.

"Yes, yes," said Mario, laughing a bit like a television Father Christmas. "I'm a very ethical person," he said, now serious and holding up a thick, calloused index finger, "and I would never cheat anybody. I rise at six every morning and read the bible for one hour. *But*, these estate agents are such parasites that I would take great delight in snatching their customers away from under their noses."

"When can I start?" asked Antonio.

"On Monday I can pick you up after I've picked up the Ecuadorian labourers from El Palmar."

"No, I'll come here in my car. It will be at your disposal."

"And you also want to do some work?"

"Of course. I can help with the labouring when I'm not tracking down the foreign customers."

"I wish I could come, but I've got classes all week," I said.

"If I line up some people, perhaps you could meet them on Saturday, Adam. If they are English, they'll like to see an Englishman involved," Antonio said in an admirably businesslike manner.

"I'd love to," I said, quite sincerely, as I felt that a second visit to Luis's house or to Pedrín's rehearsal room could wait for a while.

"So, until half past seven on Monday," Mario said to Antonio. "And I hope to see you again soon," he said to me.

We shook hands, María appeared as if by magic to say goodbye, and we headed back to Murcia.

"How do you feel about it all now?" I asked Antonio over a second coffee in the Mesón de Juan.

"Very good. Very excited."

"I can only see one problem."

"What's that?"

"That you don't really speak English."

"I've begun to learn a lot of useful phrases and questions," he said, pouring a drop of brandy into his coffee.

"Yes, but what about when they answer you?"

"We'll deal with that problem when it arises. To our venture," he said, raising his glass.

"Bottoms up," I said in English.

"What's that?"

"Just say it when you clink glasses with your English-speaking customers. They'll think you're fluent."

11

Each evening that week I arrived home to find Antonio looking increasingly tanned, tired, and frustrated at not having spoken to any foreigners. It was a baptism of fire, he told me, showing me his blistered hands, but he wanted to show Mario and his sons that he was no slacker.

"They now see that I can work just as hard as the three Ecuadorians – two labourers and one semi-skilled man – but when I visit the bars before and after lunch to look for the foreigners I feel so sweaty and scruffy in my work clothes that I don't like to approach them," he told me on Wednesday evening.

"But have you seen any?"

"Oh yes, and I've asked the locals about them. There are two English couples living in the village at present, one middle-aged and one younger couple with two small children. The older couple have retired there, but the father of the children has a taxi in London which he goes back to drive for a week at a time. Other foreigners are also to be seen looking at houses. The village is quite pretty and the foreigners have just discovered it. "

"Well, it's good that you've found all that out. Did you not try speaking to the couples?"

"The truth is that I'm worried that I won't make a good impression. As you said, I can speak to them, but I doubt that I'd understand their replies. I've heard the older couple speaking together and I understand hardly a thing," he said, smoothing the cover of the grammar book I had lent him.

"Yes, understanding is difficult, unless they choose their words very carefully. Listen, on Saturday we'll drive over and I'll try to get into conversation with them. If we get to know them it'll be easier for you to stay in touch."

"Thank you, Adam. I shall tell Mario tomorrow. He keeps asking me if I have spoken to them and says I should be more daring."

"Do you drink much, in the bars?"

"No, nothing at all. I think that's part of the problem. If I had a drink or two I'd be less inhibited, but I would also smell of drink. The Ecuadorians love their beer and can smell it a mile off. It wouldn't be fair."

"Well, a Saturday's different. You can drink a little and relax. How have you been feeling?"

"Apart from that slight frustration, very well. I enjoy the work and get on with the others. The Ecuadorians are interesting to talk to. They are here to earn money and miss their families a lot. Mario watches over us all like a father. His back is too bad for him to do much, but he likes us to work at a good pace."

"Do you think he'll pay you anything?"

"He will offer and I will refuse. We'll make our money by selling the house. We have agreed a 3% commission."

"That's good. We'll find someone to buy it."

"Yes, after we break the ice on Saturday."

On Friday evening I left Antonio poring over his English notebook and went to La Bomba for a few drinks. Pedrín was sitting at the end of the bar near the door and I managed to squeeze in next to him. I told him about the new developments and about Antonio's difficult first week.

"That's very good news," he said after graciously accepting the offer of a beer. "The work alone will be good for him, especially if he's in a positive environment. Whether the house sales are successful is a different matter. That's something more suited to you."

"But I can only go at the weekends."

"It will help. So he is at home now, studying English?"

"Yes, he wouldn't come out."

"I wish my drumming student had the same dedication," he said with a chuckle.

"Perhaps Dominic should use the method that Juan told us about in the bar."

"Oh no, he has a good job and should stick to it. He will soon find a different hobby too. Drumming is not really for him. If it was, he would have discovered that many years ago."

"How old were you when you started?"

"Practically a baby. I was always hitting boxes and suchlike. When I got a little drum as a present I would never let it go. My mother told me this, of course."

"Have you ever had a normal job?"

"Once, when I was a teenager. Since then, no."

Just then we heard the rumble of a loud motorbike approaching the pub. Troco looked out of the hatch and put his hands to his head.

"My God, another one!" he said, before slipping under the bar and out of the door.

Pedrín and I followed him out and were greeted by the sight of Dominic clad in a black leather jacket, seated astride a black Harley Davidson. He gave the throttle one last twist, took off his small black helmet, and dismounted as nonchalantly as he was able.

"Picha!" said… well, you know who said it. "First Lucky, then Luis and Chema, and now you!"

I saw that the Harley was a Sportster and that it was brand new. Dominic saw me looking at the badge.

"I decided on a Sportster to begin with because the other models are very heavy. I must get used to this one first," he said.

"Not because of the price?" I asked.

"That is also a factor, yes."

"I didn't even know that you liked bikes."

"Oh, I've always liked them. I had a Kawasaki many years ago, but I crashed it. This is a less volatile machine."

"What made you decide to buy it?"

"Oh, I was wondering whether to go out last night, but I decided to stay in. I started reading an old bike magazine and this morning I took a couple of hours off work and bought this one."

"An expensive night in," I said.

"What? Oh, well, I'll sell my car and buy a smaller one. Pedrín, how's it going?"

"Not bad. A real drummer's bike, eh?"

"Is it? Well, yes, I suppose it is. We'll have another class soon," he said, not convincing either of us. I was sure he would be joining the other Harley riders at Luis's house the next day to talk bikes.

We entered the bar and Dominic stood a round of drinks.

"Good health to enjoy the bike," said Pedrín, as Spaniards do when someone has bought a new vehicle.

"And good health to pay for it, picha," said Troco.

After a little bike talk I told Dominic briefly about Antonio's new endeavour, expecting him to view it with scepticism.

"That's good. That's excellent news. For a man who suffers from a little… strangeness from time to time it's important that he finds something to do and sticks at it. Wish him luck from me."

After another beer I walked home, happy that my two new friends were happy, each in their own way.

12

Antonio felt guilty about driving out to Villanueva on Saturday morning wearing an ironed shirt and clean jeans because Mario and his team would be working until two o'clock. I insisted that our mission was to find and speak to the English couples and that he should not dirty his hands and clothes beforehand. It was a sunny day, but high temperatures were not forecast, so I was confident that we'd see them on one café terrace or another.

We arrived at the property Mario was renovating at ten o'clock and I was disappointed by what I saw. It was a large, one-storey house on a narrow street in the centre of the village. It had a small, enclosed patio to the rear, my friend told me, but no garden. Before we got out of the car I told Antonio that it was unlikely to attract a British buyer.

"Other foreigners, I don't know, but when British people come to Spain they normally want a view and a garden at the very least," I said.

"So you think I'm wasting my time?"

I saw that the news hadn't gone down well and I strove to rectify matters. "I may be wrong, of course, and there may be people who really want to integrate into the village community; in fact I'm sure there are, and remember that we're thinking about other properties too, not just this one."

When I greeted Mario I made sure that nothing but enthusiasm showed on my face.

"It looks like you're doing a complete renovation," I said.

"Yes, I've torn out almost everything and it will be like a new house inside. I'll also clad the façade with stone and it will be the pride of the row. Come, I'll introduce you to my sons and the others."

Benjamín, a handsome lad in his early twenties, was tiling the bathroom floor with the assistance of César, a dark, wiry Ecuadorian man approaching fifty. Benjamín raised his trowel in greeting and César just nodded. They were out to finish the floor that morning and were in no mood to chat. Mario's other son, Pablo, a man of thirty with short, thinning hair, was replacing the terracotta roof tiles on a small outhouse in the patio. He smiled briefly before turning to his assistant and puffing out his cheeks.

"Come on Hernán, that mixture should be ready by now," he said.

The young, black-haired Ecuadorian had the body of a featherweight boxer, but didn't seem inclined to move it more than he had to. He greeted me cheerily and asked Mario when they could have a litre of beer.

"When you finish that roof I may bring you one," Mario said, immediately rousing the young man to greater efforts. Mario led us through a back door into the adjacent street and we stood in the shade of the wall. "The Ecuadorians like to drink beer while they work, but I don't allow it."

"Where is Esteban today?" asked Antonio.

"Poorly, they say," he said, shaking his head. "Monday is also a bad day for them. I drank a lot when I was working in Germany, and I mean a lot. I often went without sleep, but I never missed a day's work. Drink is the work of the devil and I no longer touch a drop. My wife has also put me on a diet because this is not so good." He tapped the left side of his chest. "But today we'll eat well once we have finished. So, Adam, will you speak to the foreigners today? Antonio has been a little shy with them, although he's a willing worker."

"Yes, we'll go for a coffee now and see if we can find them. Once I've introduced them to Antonio and told them to speak slowly, he'll be able to keep in touch with them and find out about other foreigners who may be looking at houses," I said, trying not to think about the nondescript dwelling behind me.

"Off you go then. We'll meet at two for lunch."

Antonio led me onto the main street and down it to a bar with a small terrace. There were a few locals inside, but the terrace was bereft of rosy or purple-faced Northern Europeans. My friend looked glum and in no condition to join in the animated conversation I planned to strike up with the first foreigner I saw.

"Have a drink," I said.

"Just a coffee."

"No, I mean a drink."

"I haven't drunk alcohol since last weekend," he said.

"That's good, that's excellent, but have a little something now. I need the old Antonio by my side this morning."

"What? The crazy one?"

"No, the lively, enthusiastic one who began this project. The work has tired you out and you need a little something."

"I'll have a brandy with that coffee then," he said, his lips twitching into a smile.

I ordered the same for me and we went to sit on the shaded part of the terrace. Antonio poured a little brandy into his coffee and lit a cigarette. He sipped the coffee to make room for some more brandy.

"I feel better already," he said, before the drink could have had the slightest effect. "I'll not worry about selling the house. If it happens, it happens, but I'm happy just to be working and learning something new."

"You'll be able to help with the electrics."

"No," he said with a shake of the head. "I'll leave that to the electrician Mario uses, a nice man from Alcantarilla. I want no reminder of the past." He finished the coffee and slid the brandy glass towards him.

"Is Mario trying to sell that house to local people too?" I asked.

"I don't know. He's on site most of the time and at lunch he talks mainly to us. He's got the idea into his head that foreigners will buy the house."

"Well, let him keep thinking that way, but I think someone local will buy it. It'll be the best house on the row. They'll like that."

"You know the Spanish well, Adam."

"I'm getting to know them. Has Mario offered to pay you for your work?"

"Yesterday he pushed four 5000 peseta notes into my hand. I put them into his shirt pocket."

"That's good, because next week I think you should work less and speak to the locals more."

"Do you think so?"

"Yes, but we'll talk about it later. Look who's coming," I said, as a tanned, grey-haired couple walked onto the terrace.

Physiognomy is a funny thing, but I immediately knew they were English rather than from elsewhere in the British Isles or Europe. They sat down at a table facing us and the sun, and when they spoke I was happy to hear that they were northerners like myself. The short, fit-looking man went into the bar and returned with a large beer and a coffee. His wife, also slight and trim, looked a friendly sort.

"Are you going to speak to them?" Antonio asked me.

"Yes, when he's drunk two-thirds of his beer. Let's talk about something else for a while because they may understand Spanish," I said, quietly and rapidly, before asking him what sort of tasks he had been doing that week.

"Mainly mixing cement and carrying bricks or tiles to his two lads, but Benjamín has already begun to show me how to lay floor tiles. He's the friendlier of the two sons and knows that I want to learn. Esteban, the Ecuadorian who didn't come today, is quite skilled, so César usually helps him while I help Benjamín."

"I see," I said, observing the interest the English lady was taking in our conversation. "It is going to be a very good house," I added, pronouncing each word clearly, before turning to face the couple.

"I couldn't help overhearing that you are English," I said as soon as they had spoken again.

"Yes, we live here," the lady said. "Your Spanish is very good."

That was all I needed. Introductions were made and we soon joined them at their table. Jack and Barbara were from Sheffield and had lived in the village for just under a year. They had both retired early – he was 63 and she 62 – and had toured South-eastern Spain until they had found an unspoilt village in which to spend the rest of their days.

By unspoilt they meant not full of foreigners. I would understand that, Jack said, because I too had chosen the Spanish way of life. They had Spanish classes twice a week, but found the grammar difficult. Their brains weren't as young as they used to be, Barbara told us, pointing to her head for Antonio's benefit.

I ordered a round of drinks – a small beer for Barbara this time – and told them what I did. They said that teaching all those people must be interesting and I agreed that it was, especially teaching my good friend Antonio.

"Adam is a very good teacher. I need English for the work I now do," he said, his long hours of study paying off.

"Yes, Antonio is working with a builder from Murcia who is restoring houses in the village," I said to them. I spoke slowly to make it clear that Antonio was to be included in the conversation. "He is working on a nice house at the top of the village now and Antonio, as well as helping with the work, hopes to help him to sell it. I guess I'm helping him to do that."

Laying our cards on the table was a risk, but if they didn't like the way the conversation was going it would be as well to know it right away. I liked them both, but it wasn't a purely social outing, after all. Their nods of interest told me that I hadn't committed a faux pas.

"It is a very pretty village. Where is your house?" Antonio asked them in English, the brandy loosening his tongue as I had intended it to.

Barbara seemed especially interested in my friend and observed his every move. "Well, the best way to show you where it is would be for you to come and see it," she said. "It's only a couple of minutes away."

We drank up and Jack led the way along the street, the muscles of his tanned shoulders flexing as he talked and gesticulated. The two large beers had put him in a good mood and he appeared glad to have met us. I guessed that despite all their efforts to integrate they sometimes felt lonely in the village.

Their house was much more like the sort of thing that Mario ought to have been restoring and a glance from Antonio told me that he was of the same opinion. It was also a one-storey dwelling with an unprepossessing façade, but the house stretched back a long way and the huge patio overlooked the deep river valley and had good views of the hills to the north and west. It wasn't an idyllic view – there were a few pylons and signs of industry – but it was theirs and they were proud of it.

"We didn't want to live out in the sticks," Barbara said. "Out in the countryside," she added on seeing Antonio's puzzled expression. "Here we've got the best of both worlds. Would you like a cup of tea, or a beer?"

We both went for the cooler option and continued to admire the view. I walked to the end of the patio and looked to the right and to the left.

"There seem to be a few houses with the same sort of view," I said to Jack.

"Yes, and one or two of them are for sale. They'll need doing up, I suppose, like this one did. Local builders did the work for us and, to be honest, I wasn't very happy with them. I had to be on top of them all the time to make sure they didn't cut corners and I had a battle about the price. I'll not be using them again."

Antonio had got the gist of this; mostly, I think, from Jack's gestures and facial expressions, and his eyes urged me to press him for more information. I chose to be subtle.

"Ha, I don't expect you'd want more Brits moving into the village, would you?"

"Oh, we wouldn't mind now. At first we were proud to be the only foreigners in the village, a bit snobbish about it really, but Trevor and Ann from London moved in a couple of months later and we were quite glad to have someone to talk to. Their two kids are going to school here now and Trevor nips back to London sometimes to earn some money in his cab. He works round the clock for a week at a time and grabs naps when he can."

Barbara brought the cans of beer and glasses and we all sat down around the patio table.

"I think that the house that Mario, the builder, is working on won't appeal to Brits or other foreigners," I said. "It hasn't got a wonderful view like yours has."

"Yes, we get a lot of visitors now," said Barbara, speaking slowly. "More than when we were living in Sheffield. A few of our friends are talking about moving out here when they retire. Is it hard work, working on the house?" she asked Antonio with a few helpful gestures.

"For me, yes. It is new work for me. This week the hands are very bad," he said, holding them up.

"Ooh, yes, a lot of blisters. Do you enjoy the work?" she asked.

"Yes, it is very good for me. I work with good people and I like use the hands," he said, getting an admiring glance from me for his surprisingly competent speech.

"What work did you both do in England?" I asked, having decided not to talk any more shop that day. Antonio could chase up the owners of the other houses on their street and the main thing was to cement our friendship with the couple.

"I worked in engineering and Barbara was a nurse," said Jack.

"It was me who wanted to retire early," she said. "My job was very stressful and it was starting to get to me. I was a mental nurse, you see." She looked at me when she said, or rather mumbled, this final phrase and I began to understand her interest in my friend, although his behaviour had been exemplary since we had met them.

We took our time over the beer. Jack told us about all the bits of DIY he was doing and Barbara tried out some Spanish phrases on Antonio.

"You must come and see us again," she said when we stood up to leave.

"I'll probably come over next Saturday, but Antonio will be here all week," I said.

She touched my friend's shirt sleeve and told him in a mixture of English and Spanish that he must call in to see them.

"Yes, I will come. Next week I work not so much and speak to people in village more. I come see you," he said, before giving her a little bow and shaking Jack's hand.

Back on the café terrace I advised against the glass of brandy that he requested with his second coffee of the morning. "You don't want to stink of drink when we meet Mario in an hour."

"Ha, today is a holiday and we've done good work this morning. I now have Barbara in my pocket. She recognised me."

"Recognised you?"

"She already knows that my head is... not quite the same as other people. I suspected that she worked in psychiatry or something similar from the way that she looked at me."

"A psychiatric nurse, she said."

"Mental nurse," he said in English. "It sounds better, I think, or perhaps worse. Ha, no matter, she is one of the good ones, like my current doctor. The women are normally more sympathetic. We'll become great friends. Jack is also a nice man and she'll now be telling him about me. I'll call round on Monday after I've located the owners of the other houses similar to theirs."

"I was going to suggest that."

"Yes, they'll be for the foreigners and the house we are working on will be for a local person."

"I was going to say that too. Should we point that out to Mario?"

"No, because if he finds a buyer we won't get our commission. I'll speak to people in all the bars and sell it myself. The price isn't unreasonable and it will be a splendid house when it's finished."

"You're becoming quite the businessman, but the commission will be for you, not us."

"No, Adam, we're in this together on all the houses that we're going to sell. Finish that little beer and I'll order you a big one."

By the time Mario arrived at just before two we were both in an excellent mood.

"You two have been in the sun, or something," he said, smiling broadly.

"We've had a very productive morning," I said. "Where are the others?"

"They've gone home. Pablo wanted to see his girlfriend. Benjamín would have stayed, but I asked him to take the Ecuadorians home in the van. I gave them a little extra rather than buying them lunch today. They don't behave well in bars," he said, before relating the story of the disastrous Friday afternoon when he had stood them beer and tapas. After the third jug of beer César had begun to cry loudly due to homesickness, while Hernán had been found sitting on the toilet with his trousers down, his head between his hands and the door wide open. Meanwhile, Esteban, the absentee, had begun to argue bitterly over their wages and suggest that he was exploiting them because they were defenceless immigrants.

"I pay them the correct rate. Since then I sometimes take a couple of litres to the site when they've finished, but no more local bars. That way I would never sell the house," he said, shaking his large head sadly.

Mario drove us three hundred yards up the street to a larger establishment and we ordered lunch. I told Mario about the morning's developments, concentrating on our budding friendship with the English couple and all the prospective customers who would soon be visiting.

"Antonio ought to stick to them like glue," I said. "Someone will come out here soon and buy the house."

"And the other couple?" he asked.

"This couple, Jack and Barbara, know them. Antonio will meet them soon."

"I have Barbara in my pocket," Antonio said with a complacent smile.

I saw that the drink was likely to make him begin to behave oddly, so I tried to steer the conversation away from him until he had eaten something. "So, the two couples and their friends are a start, but I think we need to make some leaflets in English to hand out around the area," I said, rather than mentioning the other houses on Jack and Barbara's row.

"That's a good idea," he said.

"Antonio and I will write the text before Monday."

"Good, he can tell me what you've written and then my wife can take it to the printer's near our house. How many do you think we should print?"

"Oh, about a thous-"

"Ten thousand at least," interrupted Antonio, waving his wine glass. "We will distribute them all over the region." He raised and spread his hands to indicate the vastness of the undertaking.

Fearing that his exuberance was about to spoil things, I looked at him sternly before glancing at Mario, who was smiling like a patient friar.

"Don't worry, Adam, I know Antonio at least as well as you do. Today he can relax and enjoy himself like many young people do, but on Monday he'll be ready to continue his work. This English couple's house, with the large patio and the view, sounds like the sort of thing I should be working on. Antonio, will you contact the owners of similar houses, or shall I?"

"I'll do it," he said, suddenly sobered. "From Monday I'll spend until lunchtime speaking to the English couples and the local people, and in the afternoons I'll work on the house."

"Very good. Now let's eat."

After an abundant lunch of chops, sausages and other high-cholesterol fare, we saw Mario to his car and waved him off.

"Whew, now I can relax," Antonio said, having said little during the meal.

"We'd better get back to Murcia before you drink any more."

"Yes, we'd better."

Back at La Bomba we sipped beer and jotted down some ideas for our sales leaflet until the Harley boys arrived after a short rehearsal at Luis's house.

"I shit myself on that grumpy old bastard Alberto," said Chema, dropping his little helmet onto the bar. "I shan't be going again while he's around."

"Start your own group," I said.

"No time. I'm in the lorry all week and I need to relax at the weekend," he said, pointing to the whisky and coke that Troco was pouring.

A little music talk soon gave way to bike talk, led by a still enthusiastic Dominic, so Antonio and I were left to our own devices.

"It's a pity about Dominic," he said, looking sleepy.

"What is?"

"Well, I guess his job is quite boring, so he's always looking for new ways to amuse himself. First drums, now bikes, later something else. He has no direction in life. I'm going home to rest now."

Speechless, I waved goodbye to the others and followed him out of the bar.

13

On Thursday I decided to make my evening's work at Jed's bar my last. He didn't really need me and I was fed up of pulling pints for the same old customers. I also reasoned that with the money we stood to earn from our impending house sales I had no reason to make Thursdays such a long day.

"Man, we won't see you at all then, since you've only been coming on Thursdays for a while," Jed said when he arrived at nine.

"Yes, I've been going out a lot less recently," I said, unwilling to admit that I now did my drinking in Infante. Nor did I feel inclined to tell him about Antonio's presence in my flat, or about our fledgling house sales concern. This wasn't because I feared it would flop, which I knew it well might, but because I preferred to keep my new life and my teaching life separate. Jed was a good friend, but through him the news would be likely to spread fast.

"I hope we don't lose touch," he said, swirling the contents of his beer glass before glancing up at me.

"No, I'll be round for a drink now and then when it's quiet. I enjoy seeing you, but I've got a bit bored of all the expat teacher talk."

"Tell me about it. I get it every night, man. All their grouching about students and colleagues gets so damn dull after a while. I'd like to get more Spanish folk in, but then they don't drink as much. How are your pals Antonio and Dominic?"

"They're fine. I'll bring them over sometime."

"You do that. They're wacky guys, man, and I like to see them."

"When there's a concert at La Bomba I'll let you know. You should come if you can get away," I said, knowing him to be a keen, though unaccomplished, guitarist.

"I'd sure like that," he said, his eyes resting on a table of young teachers, one of whom was guffawing loudly about something. "Keep in touch, now."

"I will."

When I got back to the flat for the first time since the morning, Antonio was sitting on the sofa with a box at his feet.

"I got the leaflets this morning, Adam. You'd better make sure there are no mistakes," he said, handing me one.

I've still got a few of the leaflets, which read as follows:

HOUSES IN INLAND MURCIA

DO YOU WANT TO LIVE IN THE REAL SPAIN?

Come and look at village and country houses in inland Murcia (the Ricote Valley, near Archena).

We are a building company (NOT an estate agency) which locates and restores houses to the client's own taste, according to a detailed estimate of the completed property.

The Ricote Valley is one of the few areas of natural beauty in South-eastern Spain where properties can still be bought at reasonable prices.

If you would like to come and see what we have already built and what else we have to offer, please ring...

Below this there was a little Spanish flag followed by Antonio's name and mobile number, and an upside down Union Jack followed by my name and number. The name and number of Mario's building company was at the bottom of the page and there was a drawing of a semi-detached house with a double garage in the top left-hand corner.

"What's this and what the hell's this?" I asked, pointing to the Union Jack and the dreadful drawing.

"Er, the picture is the best that the man at the printers' could find on the computer. It was Mario's idea to put on your telephone number. The flag was mine. Is there something wrong?"

"Well, the picture's awful, but I don't suppose they'll look at it too closely, but what if people start ringing me up all day long when I'm in class? How many leaflets are there?"

"Just two thousand, minus about a hundred that I left in the village and in Archena; in shops and bars and taped to lampposts and so forth. Have I done something wrong?"

By this time I had realised that without my telephone number on the leaflets the whole thing would be a non-starter. Antonio could say a few things in English, but would be unlikely to understand someone talking on the other end of the phone. It also struck me that if I wanted to earn a share of the commission I'd better be available to customers.

"No, I'd just like to have been consulted about putting my number on, that's all," I finally said. "Where are you going to distribute them?"

"Around all the towns and villages in the nice parts of Murcia. Anywhere where foreign people might be looking for houses. I've bought ten rolls of sellotape." He opened the box to show me.

"I assume Mario paid for the leaflets."

"Oh yes, and he's offered to pay for my petrol. He buys me lunch every day too."

"Has he offered you money for your work on the house again?"

"No, the truth is that I now spend little time working on site. I see Jack and Barbara every day and today I met the other English couple."

"Ah, what are they like?"

"Ann is a sweet lady, but Trevor is, well, a little suspicious."

"Of what?"

"Of anybody who wants to make money, I think. With Barbara's help I told them what we were intending to do and he started asking a lot of questions which I couldn't answer. I think my lack of English was a good thing because if he thinks our idea is a good one he may try something similar himself with a local builder. I got the impression that he's fed up of his weeks in the taxi and would like to make money some other way. They have a lovely village house and an expensive car, so I think he has the resources."

"We'd better avoid them on Saturday then. They'll obviously be no use to us." I picked up the leaflet and read it again. I was getting used to seeing my number on it, but I saw another minor problem.

"Is something else wrong, Adam?"

"Well, imagine I get a call from someone. What do I tell them? That we've got one house almost finished? If they came to see it they probably wouldn't like it, and then what? What have we got to show them?"

"Well, I told you that I'd spoken to one of the owners of the other houses on Jack and Barbara's street. This morning I spoke to him again and also to a lady who owns another of them. I met them again with Mario this afternoon, separately of course, and we may be able to do business with both of them."

"Go on."

"The man's house is in bad condition, but Mario thinks that he's asking too much for it. He offered to find the man a buyer on condition that the restoration work is offered as part of the package, or something like that."

"A bit vague, but it could work. And the woman's house?"

"It also needs a lot of work, but she's asking less and Mario is thinking about buying it. I promised him that we'd sell it for him," he said with gleaming eyes. "*That* is the one for us, Adam."

When I saw past the pound, or peseta, signs that were flashing before my eyes, Antonio's enthusiasm was a sight to behold. He had come a long way since I had first met him and that was more important to me than any money I might make.

"Good… No, fantastic. We'll have a look at it on Saturday and if I think it's right we'll really try to persuade Mario to buy it. *Then* I'll have something to tell people when they ring," said the man who had never sold so much as a second-hand car in his life.

"You'll like it. You're home early. How was Jed's bar tonight?"

"Quiet, and my last. I've told him I can't work on Thursdays anymore."

"Did he mind?"

No, things aren't picking up as much as he hoped and I don't think he can really afford to pay me anyway."

"Well, we'll soon be rich, but tomorrow night we should call in for a drink."

"Why?" I asked.

"Why? Because we have to leave a pile of leaflets for all those nice foreigners who go there, that's why."

"You're a genius, Antonio."

"There's a bottle of cava in the fridge."

"I'll go and get it."

14

The following night we called at Jed's bar shortly after he opened and he told us he would be happy to keep a pile of leaflets behind the bar.

"You didn't mention this last night, Adam," he said after reading our sales spiel.

"I hadn't seen the leaflets. It's Antonio's thing, really. He put my number on them just in case."

"How's your English?" Jed asked him in English.

"Not very good, but I study a lot and practise with English people in Villanueva village."

"Man, it took me a year in Spain to get that good." He gave Antonio a pat on the shoulder and switched back to Spanish. "Don't worry, when I see people come in who might have the cash to buy a house, I'll give them a leaflet and encourage them to call you."

"There'll be a commission for you if you find us a buyer," Antonio said.

"Don't worry about that," he said with a wave of his hand.

"If you find a buyer for a house that Mario owns, there will be at least 150,000 pesetas for you."

"Wow, that's a month's wages; more, the way things are going here at the moment. The next round's on me."

We drank to our bestowal of what I guessed to be a third of our commission on our American agent, had two more beers, and left. I suggested a nightcap in La Bomba, but Antonio shook his head.

"Not for me, Adam. I must be fresh tomorrow and it's unlikely that we'll find a house buyer there."

Impressed by his single-mindedness, I returned with him to the flat.

After our second Saturday in Villanueva I began to see a lot more potential in the 'Houses in Inland Murcia' project and put a sheaf of the leaflets into my briefcase for Monday. I would extract one by mistake when in the presence of my more affluent students and end up telling them all about it.

"Yes," said Antonio when I mentioned this to him, "a prospective buyer could appear from anywhere. We must carry leaflets at all times."

We had arrived in the village the previous morning under a cloudy sky and I found the cooler October weather a great relief. When I suggested a coffee on the terrace where we had met Jack and Barbara he shook his head.

"Not yet. There's a busier bar further down the street where I'm making progress regarding the house Mario is now finishing."

We entered the busy, smoky bar and the owner smiled when he saw Antonio.

"Make room for the house salesman, gentlemen," he said to the half dozen men lining the bar. Most of them acknowledged my friend and a young chap in overalls shuffled up to make room for us.

"The usual, Carlos, and the same for my English friend and colleague," he said, suddenly bright and jocular after a thoughtful walk from the car.

Two small brandies were pushed our way and two coffees soon followed. The men seemed expectant, but my friend didn't speak. He swirled his brandy, took a sip, and poured a little into his coffee.

"That will set the brain cells whirring," he said, turning to face the company. "So, which of you fellows is going to buy the best house in the village? The best house with the best stonework on the best street. Álvaro, what about you? Have you spoken to the wife yet?"

"If she wants to move anywhere, it's to a flat, the silly woman," said Álvaro, a short, tubby man in his fifties.

"A flat! There'll be no more flats built in this beautiful village," he said, shaking his finger in Álvaro's face. "Jose, a tot of whisky for this man, please. What about you, Miguel?" he asked a heavyset young man further along the bar. Miguel just shook his head and laughed.

"When the foreigners arrive to share this beauty spot with you all, the house prices will go through the roof. I want you all to get the best houses at a good price before it's too late. Only this morning I saw a coachload of Germans arriving with Deutschmarks falling out of their pockets. They will beat you to it!" he cried, before gulping down his coffee and lighting a cigarette.

"I didn't see any coaches," said a man seated at a table behind us who didn't seem to see the funny side of Antonio's theatricals.

"When you get home your furniture will be in the street, with your children on top of it," he said, nodding gravely.

"I haven't got any kids," the man growled, before turning his attention to the newspaper.

Undiscouraged, Antonio continued his banter for a while longer, introducing me to the company as he did so.

"This man knows what happens to beautiful villages like this one. He lived in Mojácar in Almería until the foreigners overran the place. He has now renounced his British passport and is about to marry a lovely Murcian girl. He wants Spanish houses for Spanish people just as much as I do. Don't you, Adam?"

"Yes, I do," I said, still a little stunned, but trying to inject some of his enthusiasm into my voice.

"We must go. There is work to be done. Mario, the best builder in Murcia, if not in Spain, will be at the house now if any of you want to secure it before the Germans get there. I'll see you all on Monday," he said, raising an imaginary hat to the company and heading for the door.

I followed him out onto the street, got into stride with him, and waited for an explanation. He had just done a wonderful imitation of his more eccentric self and I wanted to know why.

"Did you enjoy my little act, Adam?" he said once we had left the bar behind.

"Yes and no. They like you, but what's the idea? I mean, do you really expect to sell houses that way?"

"Just one house. After this first one we'll concentrate on the foreigners. What happened was this. At first I traipsed around the bars and shops telling people about our renovated house for sale on Pasos Street. They nodded, smiled, or just looked through me and I saw that I was making no impact at all. On Wednesday I had a little more wine than usual at lunch – I was starting to feel dejected – and went to that bar for coffee. That first time my behaviour wasn't an act, but they're a friendly lot and I think they were glad to see somebody different. I've decided to be a little eccentric, there at least, in the hope that word will spread about the house."

"I see, but wouldn't a potential buyer be worried about your lack of seriousness?"

"Maybe, but once they go to the house and meet Mario, they'll realise that he's a serious businessman."

"Does he know about your... tactic?"

"Yes, I told him. He says to try it for a week, but not to go over the top. Very few people have expressed interest in the house to him either, and he's willing to take the risk."

"Do you think you've had any success so far?"

"Yes, an elderly lady goes there for coffee in the afternoons and seems interested. She bought one of the new flats and has decided she doesn't like it. I told her she could call in to speak to Mario any time. Let's sit down and wait for Jack and Barbara," he said when we reached the terrace of the bar where we had met them.

We ordered two small beers and I was relieved to see him take just a tiny sip before lighting a cigarette. His demeanour with the waiter was quite restrained and I feared no repetition of his recent histrionics.

"So, once the first house is sold, will you change your behaviour in that bar?" I asked, unable to put the strange experience out of my mind.

"I don't know. It's occurred to me that my apparent craziness may have its uses in the future too. I joke about the foreigners coming to buy their houses, but they're seeing more and more of them around and they don't like the idea."

"What do they think about Jack and Barbara being here, and the other couple?"

"In general, people here like Jack and Barbara, but are not so happy about Trevor and Ann, especially Trevor."

"Why's that?"

"Jack and Barbara are friendly and try to speak Spanish. They are also retired. They think Trevor more arrogant and suspect that he'll want to set up some kind of business."

"So they like the foreigners just to live quietly and consume, rather than come here trying to make a living?"

"That's my impression, yes. So, once the first house is sold I'll probably continue to be... exuberant in that bar and begin to insinuate that I'm keen to exploit, even cheat, the foreigners. That way they may let me know when some appear, as that bar is the first one reaches on approaching the village from the interior. They've seen estate agents from out of town meet foreigners there and take them off to see properties. So, I may do that or I may take a more serious approach," he concluded.

"You've certainly put some thought into all this," I said.

"Yes, everybody does things the same way and I think one must dare to be different. In any case, most of our foreign customers will be people who call us when they see the leaflets."

"And do you really mean to cheat them?" I asked, feeling concerned about this.

"Of course not. We must build up a good reputation. We'll soon expand beyond this little village. Yesterday I distributed leaflets all around this area – Archena, Ricote, Ulea, Blanca, Abarán – and will now go further afield."

"It sounds very ambitious," I said, checking my phone for missed calls. "What about those houses you mentioned here?"

Antonio looked at his watch. "About now Mario will be speaking to the lady who wants to sell the house that I mentioned on Jack and Barbara's street. With any luck he'll have news for us at lunchtime."

Just then that amiable couple arrived and sat down with us at the table. Antonio greeted them warmly and went to order their drinks.

"Isn't he doing well?" said Barbara after watching him enter the bar.

"Yes, this house sales business looks like it might really take off," I said.

"Oh, I don't mean that. That might happen and it might not. I mean that all this activity is really good for him, up here," she said, tapping her head.

"Do you think so? You're the expert, after all."

"Yes, he's doing really well, but," she said, raising a finger, "don't expect it to last forever."

"Why not?"

"Because I'm almost sure he suffers from some kind of bipolar disorder."

"His doctors don't think so."

"Oh, what do they know? They see him once in a while and just prescribe medication. I've spent all my working life with mental patients and I know what I'm talking about."

"She doesn't think that anyone's quite right in the head," said Jack. "Even me."

"The only thing wrong with you is a touch of OCD, dear." She looked at me. "He's still scraping bits of cement off the floor tiles after all this time."

"Shoddy workmanship," he said, shaking his head.

I peered round the door into the bar and saw that Antonio was still talking to the owner. "So what can be done to prevent him from getting depressed again?" I asked her.

"You can't prevent it, as such, but if he stays motivated, takes his medication, and doesn't drink too much, he could stay well for a long time."

"And when he gets down again?"

"The important thing is for him to recognise what's happening; to know that it's not really him and that it'll pass. Getting therapy helps too."

"I'm not sure he's had much of that, but I haven't asked. I don't know if he's taking his medication either."

"Yes, since he met me he's been taking it every day, apart from one pill that only makes him drowsy. It's normally the first thing I ask him. As for therapy, well, what he's doing now is a kind of therapy too, as long as he avoids negative people. He mustn't take this house sales thing too seriously, though. Not expect too much, I mean."

Antonio returned with a large beer for Jack and a coffee for Barbara.

"We have just been talking about you," Barbara said to him in English.

"All good things, I hope. Barbara know me very well," he said to me.

"*Knows* me. Yes, I think she does," I said.

A while later we went back to drink tea on their cloudy terrace and whiled away the morning speaking a mixture of English and Spanish. Antonio hardly mentioned housing matters, so neither did I.

Just after one I got a call from Dominic.

"Adam, I must see you," he said with his usual urgency.

"I'm in Villanueva now, near Archena."

"I'll come on the bike now."

"No, no, I'm here with Antonio and the builder, doing some business."

"Can I see you in La Bomba later?"

"Yes."

"What time?"

"I don't know. I'll call or text you."

"Don't be long, Adam."

"What's it about?"

"Love. Goodbye."

I told Barbara that I'd like her to meet my friend Dominic someday, just to give him the once over, and we said our goodbyes.

Mario was waiting for us in the restaurant with a nervous smile on his face.

"Did it go well?" Antonio asked.

"Very well, I think. I made her my final offer, some of it to be in cash, and she'll give me an answer very soon. We'll finish the first house next week and I *must* sell it soon, Antonio, in order to buy materials for this new one."

My friend assured him that he had a buyer almost ready to sign on the dotted line.

"The lady from the village? Yes, she's been round twice and seems interested, but in this game you never know. Keep pushing it. I don't want to have sleepless nights."

"Don't worry, Mario," he said. "First one and then the other will be sold. Adam is also contacting all the foreigners he knows in Murcia, and we have an American friend who has a bar in the tascas. He knows hundreds of people and is telling everybody about us. On Monday morning I'll distribute leaflets in Mula, before moving on to Bullas, Caravaca and Moratalla."

"Moratalla is a long way to go to work every day," said Mario.

"We'll persuade them that the climate is much better down here in the Ricote Valley, or we'll rent a place for your boys and the workers to sleep over midweek."

"First we must sell the first house. To buy the second one is a great risk for me and I'm counting on you both to find a buyer. Don't let me down."

Mario said he couldn't stay for lunch and, after further assurances, we saw him off in his car.

"That woman's the only one who's really interested in buying the house, isn't she?" I said.

"Yes, we must pray that she makes up her mind soon."

"That was Dominic on the phone earlier. He wants to speak to me about love."

"Well, we'd better go back and see the crazy guy then."

15

After a bite to eat in the Mesón de Juan we made our way past the Chinese restaurant to La Bomba. I asked him if he'd seen May and June lately and he said that he preferred to wait until he had made a house sale.

"I want to show them that I'm capable of doing more than eating, drinking and talking nonsense," he said, looking fondly at the door.

Dominic's shiny new bike was parked near to the door of La Bomba, but the door was locked. I guessed that he would be in the Coyote and I was right. We found him seated at the bar with a slim girl in her mid-twenties by his side.

"Adam, Antonio, I'd like you to meet Cristina. Cristina, two of my good friends."

Cristina was a pretty girl with a toned body and good taste in clothes. She had shoulder-length brown hair, wore just a touch of makeup, and I felt rather envious. How did Dominic do it? Was it the motorbike? His knowledge of the works of Cervantes? Only after she had said a few words did I relax. She wasn't at all bright, so it was all right, and I stopped feeling jealous.

"Adam is one of the best English teachers in Murcia and Antonio is a judo expert," said Dominic, his arm around the girl's waist.

"That's interesting," she said with an expression of wonder approaching vacuity.

"I do karate, not judo, but I'm no expert," said Antonio.

"We also sell houses, or try to," I said.

"Houses? How interesting!" she said.

Dominic looked at her proudly, nuzzled her neck, and seemed to get a twitch in his own. He then sat up on his stool, leaned back out of her range of vision and motioned towards the door. I understood that he wanted us to step outside, but decided to make him vocalise his request.

"What do you do, Cristina?" I asked.

"I'm a student. I'm studying to be a primary school teacher."

"That's good," I said, thinking her a little old to be studying. She might have started late or she might be taking more than one year to pass each course. In Valencia I'd taught an architect who had taken twelve years to finish his degree. In the Spanish education system if you don't give up, you pass, eventually. I was no more judgemental then than I am now, but I guessed that this might be the case with Cristina.

"Adam," Dominic finally said. "Can you come over to the bike for a moment? I want to ask you something about the distributor cap."

I toyed with the idea of saying that I wouldn't know a distributor cap from a carburettor, but I relented and followed him outside. He bounded over the two lanes of the avenue and waited for me on the pavement.

"What do you think?" he asked.

"I don't know what a distributor cap is."

"No, not that. I'm not too sure either. I mean Cristina. What do you think of Cristina?"

"She's very pretty. Where did you meet her?"

"In there." He pointed across the square.

"In La Bomba? You're joking?"

"No, she was having a drink with a cousin who lives near here."

"What's the cousin like?"

"He's very friendly. Do you want to meet him?"

"Not desperately, no. What did you want to speak to me about?" I asked.

"Oh, I just wanted to know what you thought of her."

"Now you know. What else?"

"Er, well, I was thinking… You know how Antonio has a room in your flat?"

"Yes, I'm aware of that."

"Well, I wondered if I could rent one too."

"Do you want to live there?"

"Not live there, as such, but to have somewhere to go with Cristina. Somewhere private, you know."

I thought about the prospect of hearing Dominic in the throes of passion every night and didn't like the idea. On the other hand, if he took the bedroom that Antonio had rejected he would be a long way from my room. Then again, they might get down to it during the day while I was in the living room right next door. I decided to stall him.

"When did you meet her?" I asked.

"On Wednesday evening. It wasn't like me to be out midweek, so it must have been fate."

"Last Wednesday? Isn't it a bit soon to be trying to get her into bed? She doesn't look like that sort of girl," I said, giving him my most puritanical look.

"I won't be hurrying her, but if the opportunity arises... The thing is, Adam, I'm worried that when she realises how uncultured I am she'll lose interest."

"Talk to her about Don Quixote. Are you still reading it?"

"Yes, I've finished chapter seven. He's just escaped from the house and set off again with Sancho. I mentioned it and she hasn't read it, but she must be cultured in other ways. She is a student, after all."

"Oh, she seems like a down to earth girl to me. She won't get bored of you so quickly. Does she like the bike?"

"She loves it. I've already bought her a helmet and I'll buy her a leather jacket if my credit card will stand it. So what do you think?"

"All right then. Come round to the flat after lunch tomorrow and you can see the room. The sheets are quite old, so I would bring your own. I probably won't charge you anything, but there'll be a few house rules."

"Thank you, Adam. What kind of rules?"

"Like no shagging while I'm in the living room. That's the only one I can think of right now, but I'll have to consult Antonio too. We'd better go back in."

When we were approaching the others, Dominic kept up a stream of chatter about the bike, which I doubt she heard over the music. She seemed to be getting on well with Antonio, but Dominic soon reasserted his handling rights. We finished our beers and all walked over to La Bomba. It was still closed so we walked back to the Coyote.

"How does that picha expect to make the bar do well if he always opens late?" said Dominic. Cristina found this hilarious and I was sure that she wouldn't tire of him any time soon.

We returned an hour later to find Troco alone with Pedrín.

"Ah, here come the great lovers, and the estate agents," Troco said through a haze of smoke.

I couldn't remember having mentioned our house sales venture to him and he gazed at me playfully for a while before producing one of our leaflets.

"Where did you find that?" I asked.

"Three lads who go to the bar of your American friend were looking at them here last night. I had a look and saw the names. Picha, I thought, that must be my friends. They gave me one, but I don't understand a word."

"They're for our foreign customers," said Antonio.

"You should make one in Spanish too."

"We might," I said, before ordering beers for the four of us.

When the bottles of beer arrived I proffered a bank note which Troco motioned away.

"These are on Pedrín," he said.

I walked along the bar to thank him and decided to sit with him rather than watch Dominic's roving hands from such close quarters. I wondered how he had become wealthy enough to buy a round of drinks, but thought it rude to ask.

"How are things going, Pedrín?"

"Very well. We have a few concerts lined up, at last."

"Great. Where?"

"One at the Sala Gamma here in Murcia and three or four more to be confirmed. Our singer, Miguel, is taking a break from his work with Santiago and is arranging the concerts. We may also make a new record," he said, his voice as dispassionate as ever, but with a new glint in his eyes.

I wondered if he had been paid for the concerts in advance, but I thought it rude to ask that too.

"So," he said, reading my thoughts, "with money coming in soon, I can afford to be a little less careful with the little I have. How is your friend?" he asked, glancing along the bar to where Antonio didn't appear to be embarrassed by the lovebirds.

I told him where we were up to and how crucial it was for us to sell the first house.

"I hope you sell it, but it isn't good for him to get his hopes up too much. What will happen if it doesn't sell?"

"That will be a problem mainly for the builder, but Antonio has persuaded him to buy a second house in the village, so he'll feel responsible."

"That could have bad consequences for him. Is there a buyer?"

"A lady from the village. She's keen, but she hasn't made her mind up yet."

"Only her?"

"I'm afraid so."

Pedrín went to the bathroom, leaving me acutely aware of the gravity of the situation. If she decided not to buy the house, Mario would begin to have sleepless nights and Antonio would be made aware of this on a daily basis. As yet, we hadn't received a single call from anyone who had seen the leaflets and this worried me too. It was early days, but we ought to have had at least one or two enquiries. Barbara had warned me that my friend should not be subjected to negativity, but this would be inevitable if Mario saw his business in jeopardy, however diplomatic he tried to be.

Pedrín returned from the bathroom looking a lot happier than I felt.

"This American friend of yours, is he normally busy on Sundays?"

"I've never seen him on a Sunday. His wife has exclusive rights to him on that day."

"Hmm, I think you should ask him a big favour tomorrow."

"What?"

Pedrín explained his idea. After consulting with Antonio and rehearsing my supplication for half an hour I went outside to ring Jed, before having a few more beers with Pedrín, all on me, and going home.

"Jesus, Adam, you don't know how tough it was for me to get away this morning," Jed said as we drove up the dual carriageway towards Villanueva in Antonio's car. "You've gotta get me back before one or I'm a dead man."

"We really appreciate you coming, Jed, and it shouldn't take long. Just a bite to eat and a couple of beers, on us, of course."

At eleven o'clock we entered the bar in which Antonio had opted to play the extrovert and I was pleased to see it just as full as the previous day. Two familiar faces started making room for us at the bar, but we sat down at a nearby table, ordered baguette sandwiches and beer, and began to talk.

"Yes, the house on Pasos Street looks like just the thing for me," Jed said in his clear, loud, heavily-accented Spanish. "The wife and I really need to get out of that flat in Murcia at the weekends and that house is perfect."

"I'm glad you like it," I said.

"A delightful lady from the village is interested in it too," said Antonio, "but whoever puts their money down first will get it. She has only expressed interest."

"It's a lovely house and that stonework on the façade looks great. Plenty of room for the kids too."

We went on in the same vein while we ate and drank. When I got up to pay, Jed delivered his well-rehearsed finale to Antonio.

"I'm going to try to get up here on Tuesday morning. Yes, I think I'll be able to manage Tuesday morning. It's quiet in the office on Tuesdays. Get the contract ready and I'll bring a deposit."

"Tuesday it is then. We'll be at the house on Pasos Street all day," said Antonio, before standing and giving a surreptitious thumbs up to his cronies at the bar.

With two beers, a strong coffee, and a large glass of brandy inside him it wasn't hard to persuade Jed to take a little more refreshment in the bar with the terrace and the restaurant where Mario and his crew normally ate. We went through our act in each of those places just for good measure, though it was in the first bar where the local lady was most likely to hear about the big, brash foreigner who was about to snatch the house away from under her nose.

We returned to Murcia in high spirits and dropped Jed off outside his flat to face the music. He hoped that the packet of mints that he had demolished on the half hour trip back would do the trick.

"Take it easy with the wine at lunch and you'll be fine," I said.

"Let me know if our little performance does the trick, boys," he said, before disappearing into the lobby.

"Will it do the trick, do you think?" I asked Antonio.

"I think so. At least half a dozen people who know the lady were in that first bar, and village people love to pass on bad news. By tomorrow afternoon we should know one way or the other."

After another bite to eat and a couple more beers at the Mesón de Juan we greeted Dominic with great warmth when he arrived at half past three. I was surprised to see Cristina follow him in a couple of minutes later, waving her silly little helmet in greeting. Surely he ought to set up his little love nest first before he lured her into it? I guessed that his impulsivity had got the better of him.

After coffees all round and cigarettes for everybody but me, we walked round to the flat together. Our morning theatricals concluded, it now appeared to be Dominic's turn.

"Yes Cristina, I've been thinking about renting a room from Adam for some time. Nobody loves their mother more than I love mine, but I need a space where I can be myself. A place to read, listen to music and… things like that," he declaimed as we stood in the shabby lounge.

Antonio and I glanced at each other, he also hoping, I think, that Cristina was as credulous as she looked. Her vacant smile told us nothing.

"Shall I show you the room, Dominic?" I said.

"Yes. Come on, Cristina, let's have a look."

The three of us trooped next door to the large, sparsely furnished bedroom that had given Antonio the willies.

"What do you think, Cristina?" he asked her.

"Well, you'll need an easy chair, unless you're going to spend all your time in bed, but it looks all right."

Dominic sat down and bounced up and down on the mattress. "Yes, I think I'll sleep well on this. I'll sleep here sometimes, Cristina, because it's nearer to my work."

"Nearer to your work, yes," she said.

"Well, I'll leave you to have a good look," I said, before joining Antonio in the lounge.

Judging from the squeals of laughter and the creaking sounds that passed through the partition wall, Cristina was more than aware of the room's real purpose.

"I hope they don't do it while you or I are in here," Antonio said grimly.

"I've already told him about that house rule."

"If we sell the house I may buy a Harley Davidson."

"Me too."

The soon-to-be lovers emerged a few minutes later.

"Yes, we... I think it'll be fine, Adam," said Dominic. "Cristina may drop by occasionally to see me, if that's all right."

"To read Don Quixote?" I asked.

"Yes, and other books."

"To fuck like rabbits, more like," said Antonio.

As Cristina was the first to laugh, we all joined in, relieved that the little farce was over.

"Remember the house rule, though," I said, waving my finger at Dominic.

"Yes, we will read quietly."

Where to go after another happy lodger had been added to my little ménage? To La Bomba, of course. My first beer reactivated all the alcohol that I'd drunk so far that day and I decided that I'd better take it easy if I was going to be fit to see my banker student the next morning. Then I thought about the crucial event that we hoped would take place on the following day and I went outside. I took out my phone, cleared my throat, and began to ring my Monday students to cancel our classes. I had some urgent business to attend to, I told all five of them, before returning inside to inform Antonio of my decision.

"You'll lose the money, I suppose," he said.

"Yes, but I want to be there when the lady signs the contract for our first ever house sale."

"The first of many, I hope." We clinked our bottles and drank.

We only stayed until eight, both of us knowing that a hangover wouldn't make a potentially long day any easier to get through. Before leaving, I told Pedrín that we had carried out his plan and that there was no doubt that the lady would find out about her foreign competitor.

"Then you will know, one way or the other, tomorrow," he said.

"Yes."

"Good luck, but try not to let Antonio get his hopes up too much. The higher his hopes, the more severe his disappointment will be."

16

At half past eight the next morning we walked along Pasos Street in the sunshine and pushed open the door of the best house on the row. Only Benjamín and César were there, putting the finishing touches to the kitchen wall tiles. The house looked great and well worth the money Mario was asking for it.

"My father's gone to see the owner of the house that he wishes to buy," Benjamín said, putting down his trowel and lighting a cigarette. "The owner called him yesterday and it looks like we'll begin work there this week."

"That's great," I said.

Benjamín moved his head from side to side and screwed up his nose. "Is it? It's a good project, that's for sure, but I hope my father has done the right thing. He seldom buys houses, you see, as we normally do renovation work for other people. Buying that one without having sold this one is a risk," he said, shifting his gaze from me to Antonio as he spoke.

"Today the lady will buy the house," he said firmly. "Where are Pablo and the others?"

"Pablo and Hernán have gone to Pinoso in Alicante to see about a job. A swimming pool for an English couple, I think. Esteban is sick again."

"Isn't Pinoso a long way from Murcia?" I asked.

"Yes, but if this house doesn't sell we'll have to take all the work we can." He picked up his trowel and resumed work, leaving us in no doubt that he held Antonio responsible for the success or failure of the Villanueva venture.

"Shall we go and see Mario?" I asked my friend when we had wandered into the living room.

"I prefer to avoid him until I have something good to tell him," he said, looking a bit shaken after our chat with Benjamín. "Let's go to the bar to see if there is news."

We walked down the main street and entered the bar. At that post-coffee and pre-elevenses hour there were few people inside, and the lady wasn't among them.

"Good morning, Zefe," Antonio said to the young man behind the bar. "Two coffees, please."

"And a glass of brandy?" he asked, a playful smile on his lips.

Antonio looked at me and we both nodded at Zefe.

"You're quiet this morning, Antonio," he said when he had placed our coffees on their saucers in front of us.

"Yes, a little sleepy. Tell me, did Señora Muñoz come in for coffee yesterday afternoon?"

"I don't know. I left at lunchtime. So, is the American man coming to buy the house tomorrow?"

"What? Oh, yes, yes."

"That's why we wish to speak to Señora Muñoz," I said. "She may be offended if we sell the house to him without consulting her."

"Well, I know where she lives. You could call round," said Zefe.

"No, that would be intrusive," said Antonio, coming to life after drinking all of his coffee and most of his brandy. "Will she come in today?"

"This afternoon, unless she visits her sister in Archena."

"Does she often visit her?" I asked.

"Every two or three weeks, but always on a Monday afternoon."

I wondered if it would be a good idea to come clean with Zefe and tell him that we needed to know if she had heard any American-related gossip, but I was sure that Antonio would be considering this too, so I kept quiet.

He paid and we left the bar. He looked up and down the street as if wondering which way to go. I suggested that we sit down on a nearby bench and assess the situation. He consented with a nod and followed me to the bench. He sat gazing at the house fronts opposite, extracting and lighting a cigarette without taking his eyes off them.

"This is the way I see it," I said. "She may already know and might be looking for Mario as we speak. She may not know yet, but will find out this afternoon, if she comes to the bar, which she probably will. Either way, there isn't much we can do about it."

"I'll go mad if I stay here all day waiting," he said.

When someone like Antonio uses the word mad, you prick up your ears. I thought for a while. By the time he had lit another cigarette I had something to say.

"Listen, why don't we go to Jack and Barbara's and just take it easy there for a while? They might know something."

"I doubt it, and Barbara will make me more nervous by telling me not to get worked up and not to be disappointed if the house doesn't sell. If the house doesn't sell all this is finished for me. I won't be able to face Mario after putting him in this situation."

"Nonsense. He knows the score and if he's talking to the owner of the second house now it's because he's prepared to take the risk. Personally, I would wait, but if he buys it, that's his business. Anyway, if the lady doesn't buy, somebody else might come along."

"How many calls have you had since I began to distribute the leaflets, Adam?"

"Er, none."

"Exactly the same as me. None at all, not even one. You'd think one or two people would have called."

"Let's go for a walk. It'll help us to think."

Much has been written about the therapeutic value of walking and by the time we had completed a circuit of the village and arrived back at the same spot I was in a position to endorse this point of view. We had walked at a good pace and hadn't spoken at all, but when we sat back down on the bench I saw that Antonio was smiling again.

"Of course, all we have to do is go back into the bar in half an hour when the men are having their elevenses. At least one of them will know if she came in yesterday afternoon and if she got the news," he said, his eyed lively again. "If she wasn't there, I think I'd prefer to return to Murcia, have lunch at the Chinese, and forget about the whole thing."

In the event, we didn't need to re-enter the bar to find out if she had been there the day before, because Álvaro, one of the most assiduous regulars, stopped by the bench.

"What, Antonio, taking the air?" he said, with a brief nod in my direction.

"Yes, Álvaro, we're just about to have a bite to eat," my friend replied. "Did you take coffee in the bar yesterday afternoon?"

"Always."

"And was Señora Muñoz there?"

"I don't think so, no, I didn't see her."

Rather than collapse in a heap on the ground, as he might well have done an hour earlier, Antonio's smile did not leave his face. He turned to me and I could see that he'd had an idea.

"I'm a little worried, Álvaro, because the American man is coming to buy the house tomorrow. If I don't tell her, she'll be very offended. She's a nice lady and I don't want to upset her."

"I know where she lives," the man said. "You could call round there."

"Yes, yes, but I fear that if I do that she'll think that I'm trying to pressure her. I would rather see her in the bar, or for somebody else to tell her."

Álvaro's normally bland face creased into an expression which looked very much like cunning. "You don't want to pressure her, eh?" he said.

"No, it wouldn't be right," my friend said.

"So you just want her to find out that the American has been here and is keen to buy?"

"Well, yes."

"That American will not buy so much as a cucumber in this village. I saw you approach the bar yesterday when I was walking up from my house. The three of you seemed like great friends, talking and laughing together, not at all like house salesmen with their customer, ha, ha!"

"It's true that we've known each other for some time," I said, rather lamely.

"Come, let's go back to Murcia," said Antonio, beginning to push himself to his feet.

"Wait a moment, Antonio. There is something we can do," said Álvaro, resting a hand on his shoulder. "I don't like estate agents, generally speaking, but I like you and would like to see more of you around here. You brighten up that boring bar."

"What could you do?" I asked.

"I could go and see her now. She is my wife's cousin and I know her well. I could go and see her and tell her that an American is going to buy the house tomorrow."

"Would you do that, Álvaro?" Antonio asked him.

"Well, I take it that you aren't selling the house out of the goodness of your heart?"

"No."

"I cannot work, you see, due to my back, and I only receive a small disability payment each month. 20,000 pesetas would be a great help to me."

"If the lady buys, it's yours," said Antonio, standing and grasping his hand.

"I'll go and see her now. Meet me in the bar in half an hour." He stretched his back for good measure and walked away up the street.

After Antonio had smoked yet another cigarette we entered the bar and sat down at a quiet table in the corner. He just wanted a brandy, but I insisted that we have a bite to eat.

"She could appear at any time during the day," I said. "You mustn't be drunk when she does."

We had just finished our sandwiches when Álvaro walked in. He looked glumly in our direction, ordered a short drink at the bar, and shuffled across the room towards us. He put down his glass, took a seat, and sighed.

"Well? Did you see her?" I asked.

"I saw her."

"Did you tell her the story?" Antonio asked, clearly fearing the worst.

"I did. I spoke of other things and then mentioned it casually."

"What was her reaction?" I asked. "It doesn't look like she was bothered by the news."

"No, she wasn't bothered at all."

"So all is lost," said Antonio, nodding slowly.

"She wasn't disturbed by the news, but have you ever seen me order a large whisky at this time of day before, Antonio?"

We both looked at him, at the glass of whisky, and at each other.

"So...," I began.

"So she picked up her handbag and went out to find your builder friend," said Álvaro, that poker face of his breaking into a broad smile. "'No American son of a bitch is taking that house from me,' she said as she left. I've never heard her swear before."

"Zefe!" Antonio cried, before holding up Álvaro's glass. "Three more of these over here, please."

As nothing had been signed yet, I made sure we kept the celebration discrete and urged my friend not to order any more drinks before we had seen Mario. He nodded in agreement before holding up three fingers to Zefe and slapping me on the back.

"Relax, Adam, that 3% is ours for sure." He took a swig of whisky. "Success is ours," he said, before clinking my glass and Álvaro's.

I made a rough calculation of 3% of what I believed the sale price to be and wondered if it really warranted such jubilation. Still, I'd decided that Antonio would be keeping most of it. After paying Álvaro and giving a little something to Pedrín, Jed and my good self it would be a nice bonus on top of his benefits. I hoped he wouldn't make a down payment on a Harley.

Antonio took his time with his second whisky as Álvaro seemed to be feeling the effects of his third. My friend ordered three cigars, one of which I put in my shirt pocket, and they puffed away contentedly.

"Álvaro, my friend, I will bring you not 20,000 but 40,000 pesetas as soon as I have it and I'll also buy you the best lunch the village can offer," Antonio said. "And we can do more work together. You can watch out for the foreigners who come in here with the estate agents and let me know. You can count on one good commission every month, at least."

He appeared to have forgotten that we hadn't received a single call after littering the whole area with our leaflets, but now wasn't the time to remind him of that. After I had put him off at least three times, he insisted on calling Mario. The instant he relayed the good news to us – she had put 100,000 pesetas down and signed a preliminary contract – my primary concern was getting him, and me, back to Murcia before he got too drunk to drive.

In the event he was more responsible than I had given him credit for. Before meeting Mario we called in to see Barbara and Jack to tell them the good news. They were both genuinely pleased, but Barbara, as expected, told him not to get his hopes up too much.

"You have sold one house, and that is very good," she said slowly in English. "But it might not be so easy to sell another one."

"I not care," he said, before sipping from the can of beer that Jack had given him.

"I *don't* care," I corrected. "What do you mean, you don't care?" I asked in Spanish.

"I don't care because *that* was the house I wanted to sell. I wanted to achieve something and I've done it. I'll try my best to sell more, of course, but I'd like to spend more time working with Benjamín and learning from him."

I translated this for our hosts' benefit and the three of us smiled with relief and pleasure, none more so than Barbara.

"That is good. Working with your hands is good for your head," she said to him with appropriate gestures.

He walked around the table, took her by the shoulders, and kissed her on the forehead. "I know, I know. Money is not important," he said. "If my head good, everything good."

It later became apparent that filthy lucre really wasn't the first thing on his mind. After tracking down Mario to the house on Pasos Street, the builder was as anxious as I was for us to return to Murcia before lunch.

"Take the rest of the day off, super-salesman," he said.

"Tomorrow I'll be here in my working clothes," Antonio said.

"Good, we'll see if you are tougher than some of the Ecuadorians, ha, ha," Mario replied, ushering us towards the car.

On the drive back to Murcia we both found that making mental calculations took the edge off the whisky and beer we had drunk.

"Fifteen million pesetas she's going to pay for the house," said Antonio.

"So 3% will be… 450,000 pesetas."

"That's what I reckon too. 40,000 for Álvaro leaves 410,000. Even after we've given Pedrín and Jed a little something – say 30,000 to each of them – it leaves us both with a nice sum of money."

"No, no, I don't want half," I said. "I've done no more than the others, so give me the same as them."

"Adam, have you ever fallen from a car at 110 kilometres per hour?"

"Not that I can remember."

"Then don't speak such nonsense again. Without you none of this would have happened. I would have been sitting in the Coyote now with all my stupid things in front of me."

"Without Adam here I would have been sitting in the Coyote now with all my stupid things in front of me," Antonio told May and June as they stood side by side behind the spare chair in the restaurant later that afternoon. "Now I have sold a house and I feel *fantastic*!"

This exclamation made the man at the table across the aisle jump, but only earned my friend a mild rebuke.

"That's good, but don't spend all evening in those stupid bars. *And* I don't want to see you in here again any day except Saturday or Sunday," said May, sounding like the good, strong wife and mother that I believe she later became.

"You will only see me at the weekend, I promise," he said, reaching over to pat her hand.

"And make sure you get up for work tomorrow," said June.

"You can be sure of it."

We did spend the evening in those stupid bars and he did get up for work the next day. I thought about him sweating out the toxins on the building site while I was striving to look cheerful before my class of primary school teachers. I envied him, but I didn't mind.

Epilogue

This seems like just the right time to bring these reminiscences to a close, but I won't leave you with one of those maddening cliff-hangers.

I stayed in Murcia for another year, during which time I met a girl and eventually moved to her home town in Andalusia. Antonio carried on living mostly in the flat and working with Mario and his sons, but never sold another house. The only thing the leaflets produced were a few weird calls and a modest piece of restoration work on a house in Ceutí, but Mario sold the second village house to a man from Murcia and they always had plenty of work. By the time I decided to leave Murcia, Antonio was on Mario's payroll and soon found himself a neat studio flat, also in the Barrio del Carmen, but closer to the river.

After they had finished their work in Villanueva, he stayed in touch with Jack and Barbara and drove round for a pep talk every now and then. He told me by email that he had become a pretty handy semi-skilled man, his work interspersed only by occasional periods of mild depression. A few months after I left he met a girl, but things didn't work out. We lost touch after a few years, as men do, but I like to think that he is still working with his hands, as I am sure that rewarding manual work among positive people was what he needed all along.

Pedrín's group played a few concerts before he returned to his life of resigned penury until more concerts came up. This cycle continued for some time, but judging from Los Marañones website, as seen in December 2014, things have picked up in the meantime and it appears that he is working more regularly now. He has also lost the huge beard and ragged ponytail and now looks like the thoughtful, considerate gentleman that he was then too. He isn't smiling on the website photos, but I'm guessing that he will have done something about those missing teeth as well.

Jed battled to make the bar pay for another year, before selling the business for a modest sum and joining the ranks of language teachers, despite his lack of qualifications, and doing rather well at it.

Troco's bar also bit the dust and he went to work with his brother-in-law as some kind of salesman.

And Dominic? Well, his stay in my flat was a short and sporadic one and his relationship with Cristina lasted for three or four months. When he told me he was ending their relationship because he didn't find her stimulating enough, you could have knocked me down with the proverbial feather, but that's Dominic for you. We kept in touch via text messages and the occasional call, until one day his number was 'no longer available' and that was that. I don't know if he ever finished Don Quixote.

As for me, well, those hectic weeks got me out of the expat language teaching circle once and for all, and I always look back with great fondness on those special friends who helped me to do it.

Printed in Great Britain
by Amazon

46093362R00086